Andy Kent is the third child of a large English family, and has lived every day of his life as if it was his last. For someone that has lived on the edge, Andy has been successful in the two main areas of life; as a family man, giving life to two children that he was told he could not have, and building a business that provided for his family. He has also given others the knowledge and understanding to be able to help themselves. He has cheated death several times only to come back stronger.

Andy Kent

WHITE LIGHT

AUSTIN MACAULEY PUBLISHERS™

LONDON • CAMBRIDGE • NEW YORK • SHARJAH

A CIP catalogue record for this title is available from the British Library.

ISBN 9781398435858 (Paperback)
ISBN 9781398435865 (ePub e-book)

www.austinmacauley.com

First Published 2022
Austin Macauley Publishers Ltd®
1 Canada Square
Canary Wharf
London
E14 5AA

Every book takes hard work and dedication from many people, not just the subject. So I would like to say thank you to my family, in particular, Jan, for supporting me in this venture and being happy for me to share our story – thank you, from the bottom of my heart.

Thank you to Alison Folwell, for helping my words to flow and make sense, and shaping this book into something I shall enjoy reading, time and time again – there were so many memories, it was hard to know when to stop!

To my brilliant team, at Andy's Kars – what would have I done without you all.

And of course, a final thank you to you, the reader of this book. Thank you for taking the time to read my story. I hope the prevailing message you take away from it is one of hope; that no matter what your circumstances, no matter what life throws at you, you always have a choice to make life worth living. Never give up – there is always something worth fighting for.

Table of Contents

Some old family photos

The day grandfather retired from working at the Prudential.
He is the one on the right.

Mum and Dad – 1953 wedding.

Grandmother and Grandfather Gerrie – 50th wedding Anniversary.

Foreword

It isn't everyone who can say they've survived death. The first time the hospital called, I dropped everything and ran. He didn't have much time left, they told me; I should come in as quickly as possible. And I did – Maple Cross, Rickmansworth to Maida Vale Hospital near Edgware Road. Even back then, it wasn't a quick journey, and that day it felt interminable. When I got there, he looked just the same. Sleeping. I knew he wasn't sleeping – I knew he was in a coma. A few weeks before, he'd suffered what they call a cerebral haemorrhage. A brain bleed. Most people don't survive from the damage inflicted on the brain, but Andy had. But then, when they were treating him afterwards and trying to find out what had happened, they pumped him full of iodine dye to monitor what went on. Unfortunately, as it turned out, Andy was allergic to iodine, and it sent him into a coma. A coma which killed him.

But not that day. That day, he was sent home again. He had stabilised, and they weren't so worried. And, strange as it may sound, I wasn't that worried either. I knew Andy. Andy was a fighter. I knew he wouldn't give up, so I refused to accept that he might die. I just *knew* he wouldn't.

So, the second time I got the call, I went, but not in such a rush.

And sure enough, he turned out to be OK.

By the third time, I was bordering on complacent about it. I was in the middle of cooking dinner when the phone rang, and I'd be damned if I was going to waste it. So, I finished cooking it, sorted the children out, and then made my way over, a lot more calmly. It was getting a bit annoying, truth be told, slogging all the way to the hospital, all the time, to watch my husband just lying there.

This time was a bit different, though. Because this time, he died. I didn't believe it. I couldn't believe it. This was Andy, Andy Kent, the most stubborn, obstinate man I had ever met. The man who had refused to accept six years before, that he only had two years to live. The man who had spent more time in hospitals than my entire family put together and was still smiling. The man I married. The father of my children – children, I found out sometime later, he'd been told he wouldn't be able to have. *That* Andy couldn't be dead. They must have got it wrong.

And funnily enough, they had.

But I'll let Andy tell you all about that.

JAN KENT

Introduction

Welcome to the world, Andy Kent.

I've never taken the easy route. I was even born two weeks early, taking everyone by surprise, on Sunday 21st July 1957. My mum, having already had two children before, spent the first few hours of the 20-hour labour running up and down the stairs to get things moving faster – even back then, I was stubborn, with a tendency to worry people. When I was born, at home rather than in hospital, the umbilical cord was wound around my neck, making me an alarming shade of blue, but by all accounts, I was bright and alert and ready to face the world. I weighed in at a very respectable 9lb 4oz.

The doctors informed my mother that I had both asthma and eczema pretty early on, just the first in what would become a long list of medical issues.

My first photo at age nine months with my older brother and sister,
Sandy and Sue.

Now, I know that there is probably no such thing as a
"normal" family, but mine was certainly a bit different from
most. I remember the house we lived in; 32 Kimpton Place in
Garston, Watford. My father, David, was a printer, and my
mother, Geraldine, was dedicated to her own children and the
many she fostered. Over the years, my family grew and grew,
the numbers constantly changing with the seemingly constant
ebb and flow of foster children, and I had plenty of siblings
too. My older brother Alexander (Sandy, to most) and sister
Susan were joined by many more – there were six of us boys,
with Don, Gavin, Victor, Amadin (a long-term foster child)
and Simon as well as Sandy and me. My parents adopted three
girls too, Ro, Pet and Gerry, after fostering them for a long
time. Mum fostered over 700 children during my time at home

– we were quite a sight walking around town, on our way to church or school. We were referred to as the Kent Clan and even as Doctor Barnardo's children.

This was my family when I was ten years old, in 1967 at church.

I always enjoyed church back then, and Sunday was probably my favourite day of the week. There was something about it that really appealed. I loved listening to the minister giving his sermons and was always a bit envious of how everyone hung on his every word. How I wished I could get people to listen to me like that! No one bothered me when we were at church, everyone was listening, staring straight ahead and concentrating, so it was, to me at least, a peaceful place and one I felt comfortable in. However, I could still get myself into trouble. One day, I was playing with the bell ringers' hand practice bells and nearly jumped out of my skin when the Minister came in – resulting in me splitting my eyebrow open, needing seven stitches! We must have been quite a sight, taking up so much space just for one family. But it was important to my parents that we always went, even on Christmas Day.

Christmas was always a happy time in our house. I remember so clearly the magic of that day, how we always pulled together to make happy memories, no matter what arguments might have gone on before. On waking, we'd each find a sock filled with little bits and pieces which we could look through before going downstairs for breakfast. Then it was church. We attended St Stephen's Presbyterian Church on Clarendon Road, Watford, and when we got back, we all tucked into hot mince pies with hot milk while Mum and Dad had either coffee or sometimes a glass of sherry with neighbours that popped in to wish us a Merry Christmas. Then, and only then, would Dad unlock the lounge door (he never trusted us to leave the presents alone, so he always locked the door), and we would all pile in to find our presents.

Dad would have the Super 8 film camera and take photos of us as the room turned into a chaotic hive of activity as we delved excitedly through the presents to find our own. But however much of a rush we were in, we always worked together, making sure the younger children got their gifts first, and everyone did their bit, so no one had to wait too long, though it always felt like an eternity before my turn came. It was such a happy home on Christmas Day, and I wished that all the days could be like that. Not for the presents necessarily, though of course, that was great. But more, it was the feeling of truly being a part of the family, being loved, being a part of something whole. Because for a lot of the time, I felt like such an outcast.

Born with asthma and eczema, I'd had health problems all my life, and those were just the tip of the iceberg, though of

16

course, I didn't know that to start with. I was always accident-prone – if there was something to trip over, I'd be the one tripping over it. If blood were spilt, it was nearly always mine. I could wake up in the morning with bad nose bleeds that had started during the night based on the amount of blood, walk down the stairs, fall, splitting my head on the bottom newel post and not know how this happened! I was always mucky, always the last to get dressed, and always the first to be injured during any game or outing.

Sandy and I were both allergy-prone too and spent a lot of time going up and down to London, to St Mary's Hospital, for tests. But while we both had allergies and needed medical help, he didn't have the added complications of eczema. It was awful, eczema. It got so bad at times that I would sit down and feel the boils bursting on the backs of my leg, or I'd bend my arms, and the scabs in the pits of my elbows would split open and start to bleed. It went on like that my whole childhood, and of course, made school even worse than it was already. It was just another reason other children made up horrible nicknames for me and teased me about my skin. The boils that developed at the backs of my knees, in my armpits and in the creases of my elbows were agonising – both physically and emotionally. But of course, the treatments at that time were minimal, and although I spent so much time in hospitals, no one seemed to be able to do much to help.

It wasn't just eczema. Sometimes I felt like I had some kind of plague, like I was cursed to suffer one problem after another. One thing would clear up, but another would get worse in its place. The asthma was really debilitating too – not only was it a serious health issue and meant yet more time in hospital, but it also stopped me from running around with the others, from joining in with playground games. If I'd ever been invited to in the first place, that is. Maybe if things had been different; maybe if *I* had been different. So, I felt more and more detached from my family, the runt of the litter, the second-rate citizen. My brothers and sisters were all far cleverer than me; they did well at school and had brains. I just couldn't catch a break. I felt like such a disappointment to my parents, particularly my father.

I always found it hard to speak to him and felt he saw me as very much second best. Years later, after he had died, his second wife took great pleasure in telling me that he'd only ever really seen Sandy as his real son, as the first born. Of course, I'd sensed that all my life, but hearing it out loud will never cease to hurt. I remember wishing even back then that I had a dad who would listen to me and who could see the real me, not just the sum of my illnesses, my accidents, and my behaviour. I was a very affectionate child, always wanting cuddles with Mum, always wanting love. But with so many children in the house, there wasn't always enough to share, and despite the busy home I lived in, I spent a lot of my childhood feeling very lonely.

Having so many of us meant that we were always crowded. I was so excited the day we moved to a bigger house in Garston Lane, number 23. It was across one road and around the corner from the old place, and we all helped, a long line of worker-ants carrying things from the old house to the new one. Instead of three bedrooms, we now had four, as well as a bigger garden, kitchen and lounge. We still had to share, of course – there were 17 of us at that time – but it was a great adventure all the same. It was hard to find a quiet corner to yourself, though, with all those children around, and I used to long for some space of my own.

This is where I spent my childhood – Garston Lane, Garston, Watford. 1964–1975

Our holidays were always chaotic, with such a crowd, but we had a lot of fun. It was always camping, sometimes just for a weekend, sometimes for the whole summer holidays – the full eight weeks as it was back then. We'd load up the old van and trailer with a never-ending pile of bags, and tents and sleeping bags, and it took forever to get to the camp site. Then we'd have to spend all day setting up the tents and getting organised – even as a kid, it seemed like a lot of hard work, so I can only imagine how much work it involved for my parents. With so many of us, there were plenty of laughs and good times, but it had its bad points too. There was no privacy, and with my poor health, it was never the most comfortable experience. I look back on it mostly with fondness, but I remember wishing even then that things could be different. Compared with real life at home, though, and school, in particular, it was positively heavenly.

Halcyon days and harsh realities

Those camping trips were one of the biggest highlights of my childhood. Some of the details have blurred over the years, of course, but there are episodes that still stand out as clearly as if they'd happened last week.

It was quite the operation, taking so many of us on holiday. We'd set up camp first, Mum and Dad in a sort of main, hub tent, with the youngest of the children in with them. This was HQ, the mess tent – where we'd eat, report back to prove we were still alive and so on. Dinner times were often chaos, and we all had to muck in, sitting around as a group peeling entire sacks of potatoes and having to trim the peelings if Mum thought we'd taken off too much skin. We didn't mind though, chores were always just part of our lives growing up, and with so many of us, it just couldn't have worked any other way. Sometimes things got very messy, though, with so many youngsters around – the sight of little Amadin sitting there with his upturned porridge bowl on his head, with porridge dripping down his face is one I'll take with me to the grave. Given his tight curls, that porridge was almost impossible to get out as well – we laughed and laughed. Well, all except for Mum, for some reason.

Our own tents were satellites around the main hub, six or seven smaller tents shared by varying numbers of us. We were always off on adventures, doing what we liked. As long as we looked after the younger ones and stayed out of trouble, we were pretty much free to roam.

Donavan always loved climbing trees – except perhaps for the time he fell out of one, landing on a branch awkwardly so that it skewered his leg all the way through. So much blood – we all found it hysterically funny, seeing him there on the ground with this big twig stuck through his leg... Mum's shrieks were not quite so funny, and we weren't too popular for laughing, but at the time, it was all just part of the big adventure. I'm sure it looked worse than it actually was... There were no lasting effects apart from two small scars, but it was pretty dramatic, that's for sure.

Sometimes Mum and Dad would take us all to the beach. We were such an assortment of ages and appearances and such a big group that people sometimes thought we were from a charity or something, like Dr Barnardo's. Once in a while, a stranger would come up and kindly offer to buy us all an ice cream, which was such a rare treat. Mum and Dad were strict and proud people and would never accept handouts, but if we were on holiday and someone had offered, and they were in the right mood, just occasionally they'd accept, and we'd all get ice cream. Moments like that were few and far between, but wow, they were worth waiting for. Now a tub of ice cream does not last long.

We learned a huge amount from those camping trips, real-life skills that I've carried forward to this day. I remember one campsite in particular, just outside Poole in Dorset, located on a steep hillside, and the weather was terrible. Back then, groundsheets weren't an integrated part of a tent and weren't particularly waterproof, so if the rain came down while you were camping on a hill, you'd end up with a river running through your tent. So, we'd dig trenches around the tent, like a moat, to deflect the water and keep our stuff dry. We learned about all the equipment, about food preparation and so on. Really great stuff that's been useful ever since.

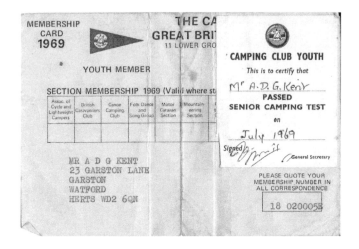

Chores were a part of our daily life at home, of course too. Mum had her planner up on the wall, with each of us assigned different jobs each day – washing up, drying, cleaning, tidying, food preparation, taking out the bins. It was essential and expected that we help out, and of course, we did.

Of course, having so many children around, my parents had to keep us in check. Children will be children, and we were no strangers to mischief. Discipline was strict. Sometimes, when we were all punished for the actions of just one, we felt it was all very unfair, real rough justice. Times–like when all the boys lined up, with our pants down, bent over the bench seat, and our dad took his belt to us, just because one of us had taken the dinner money from the shelf, where it was put out for Monday morning. The girls would get the cane across their hands. Naturally, there were times when we all really had been involved, but if we were punished for something just one of us had done, it never went down well. Being so accident-prone, I was often in trouble and was no stranger to the punishments my dad would hand out. It was always black and white to them, and neither Mum nor Dad was ever interested in excuses or real reasons, which is what I find still later in life. There is never room for compassion; or acceptance when someone just wants to say thank you, it is always seen as having a secret agenda. Any protests we made were always ignored – after all, we were just children, so why should we be listened to? I learned early on what right and wrong looked like through my parents' eyes, but I'm not sure we were always in agreement.

It can't have been easy, looking back, having to take me to and from the hospital so often. At the time, of course, it didn't really occur to me that it might be putting anyone else out – I was the one suffering, and I didn't get a lot of sympathy. To this day, my body is covered in scars, and I've visited more hospitals across the country than I care to remember. Mostly the visits were for cuts and abrasions – I was always falling over or banging into things, and my injuries were usually quite serious. Added to that were the severe asthma attacks, which put me in hospital several times. When I was ten, I developed a large lump on my left knee, which grew so much that eventually, I couldn't bend my leg at all. This was to the extent that Mum had to get me around in a pushchair. I saw doctors about it and was recommended surgery.

I was nervous about the operation, and I don't remember much about it except that it was ten days in the hospital and six weeks with plaster from my groin to my ankle. That operation was a scary experience, but I just wanted my knee to work again, so I could walk and run like everyone else. I wasn't given any explanation for the lump, and to this day, I have no idea why it grew or what caused it. Little did I know then that it was to be the first of 17 operations throughout my life just on that one knee, culminating in it being totally replaced at the age of 40. I'm glad I didn't know that then; as it was, I just kept going and accepting whatever the doctors told me, going through my history of medical issues every time I saw a new one, and knowing that I would never get any real answers.

When I was 13, I collapsed and was admitted to St Thomas' Hospital, London, with severe bleeding from my kidneys. They continued to bleed, and I was subjected to all sorts of tests over the next few years. It had a lot of knock-on effects on my weight, which fluctuated enormously, to my general wellbeing (or lack of it) and tiredness. The doctors have never given me a satisfactory answer, and to this day, my kidneys continue to evade medical diagnosis. But they're hanging on in there, at least for now, so they obviously know what they're doing even if no one else does. St Thomas' played a huge part throughout my teen years.

Although I never knew any differently, I knew I was different. None of the others had the constant medical needs that I did; none of them struggled to breathe or had skin they could never find comfort within. I've only ever had my own experience, but I grew up surrounded by hundreds of other healthy children, only ever getting a tiny slice of my parents' time. I felt inadequate – and school would only make that feeling a whole lot worse.

Chapter One
Education, Education, Education

I get the impression that most people look back on their school days with at least some fondness. These days I am devoted to learning and do as much of it as possible, both for myself and in terms of helping others to learn, so it seems strange looking back at how much I hated it. School itself was not a happy time for me. Of course, my illnesses didn't help. Children, as any of you who have them will know, can be cruel and not always intentionally so. Even if well-meaning, they lack tact and diplomacy, and I was already uncomfortably aware of my skin condition and breathing difficulties before I ever went to school. Unlike my brothers and sisters, I could not read and write before I went to school, so I felt I was starting on the back foot, but I hoped to learn when I was there.

So off I went to Garston Infant School. I must confess my memories of it, in general, are hazy, and perhaps there were some fun times mixed in, but I have three very clear memories which cloud everything else and became the foundation for my hatred of school.

I was not blessed with the brains the rest of my family seemed to take for granted. Reading and writing did not come easily, and I found it incredibly hard to concentrate on the work. These days, fortunately, dyslexia is often spotted early, and special measures can be taken to help a child who has it, but back then, it wasn't acknowledged or even known about by many. The teacher's assumption was, therefore, that I was either stupid or not working hard enough – or perhaps even both. A regular pain or disobedient child. Sometimes this still happens today. I was, therefore, frequently in the corner, the humiliating D hat on my head, singled out for my stupidity. Most five-year-olds these days don't really experience much in the way of embarrassment, but I remember it with crystal clarity. A dunce. That was me, Andy Kent, the runt of the litter, a dunce of the class. And I hated it.

Writing with your right hand was the way we were taught, but it never felt comfortable to me. Far more natural was the urge to use my left hand, where the pencil sat better, where I felt in control. In my right, the pencil was alien, awkward. I couldn't hold it correctly, and I certainly couldn't write with it. Yet another example of my stupidity, or so it seemed to me, and the teachers did what was quite normal back then to train me out of such a "bad habit" – they tied my left hand behind my back, so I could only use the right one. Restrained not only by my lack of understanding of the words but also physically by the ties they used, I felt punished for what only felt natural. I hadn't decided to be left-handed – I just was. But that wasn't how things were done, and so each day, they'd tie my hand back until I stopped trying to use it. I ended up stiff and sore, but mostly just frustrated and resentful. My second memory of an early education, which did nothing but teach me what I couldn't do.

I knew lots of other children at school, and many were those my mum would take care of, either through fostering or out of school care. Usually, it was an advantage, having so many foster brothers and sisters; it was an unspoken understanding that we'd stick together, stand up for each other, and act like a proper family. Racism was common back then and openly shared, and of course, many of our foster siblings were from different cultures or countries. We attracted a lot of attention, that's for sure, but mostly it was good to have so many people having your back, just as we made sure we had theirs.

But it didn't always help, and accidents always befell me. One day I was playing with a girl, who my mum looked after, out in the playground. Rosemary Frazer, she was called, and I will never forget her. It was a physical game we were playing, spinning each other around and around until we were dizzy. It may well even have been fun – it certainly sounds like it to me! But as I was swinging around, somehow, I banged into her, and her front tooth was knocked out. I don't remember whether it had been wobbly before, nor whether there was much blood. What I remember is that she said I'd punched her. And I remember being marched off to the headmistress, Mrs Carr. And I remember getting the cane for it. Aged just five or six, I was beaten for an accident that had not been my fault – and it hurt. It hurt so much I wet myself – and had no other clothes to change into, so I had to stay in those wet clothes all day. I imagine the other children had yet more laughs at my expense for that, but I don't remember. My embarrassment was too great, and I wasn't paying attention to them.

My heart goes out to that little boy who just wanted to be cuddled and looked after and told everything would be OK. Except that it wouldn't not really, and perhaps it was better that he knew that from the start. What would I say if I could speak to myself then? "It's a tough road ahead for you, Andy, my boy. But you can do it. You can do it. Nothing and no one is going to beat you down because you will always get back up again. I believe in you."

I'd love to cheer things up now and tell you how it all got so much better, that I got used to school and school got used to me, how we learned to get along, but unfortunately, things didn't get much better in junior school. I went to Lea Farm School, and I was put in the lowest class, where I still struggled with the basics of reading and writing. My class teacher was actually a friend of Mum's, someone whose children she looked after from time to time. Rather than give me any special treatment, though, she singled me out all the more, making an example of me because I still could not read or write. I spent more time outside that class or in the corner wearing the hated dunce's cap than I ever spent learning at a desk. The other children saw the way I was treated, and so I was an easy target. The bullying that started then carried on and lasted all the way through school. They called me names because of my eczema, and if I hadn't felt like the village idiot before, I sure as hell did then.

Eventually, I was moved into Mr Gammon's class. I was pleased at first, as I'd heard he had a great deal of patience with people like me, and I began to hope that finally, I might start to learn something and not be singled out. How wrong I was.

At home, when she was on the phone, my mum would take notes. She used shorthand, which she'd learned some years before, and I was always fascinated by it, all these strange letters and symbols and squiggles which made perfect sense to her, but to me, were an indecipherable code, a mystery. But she wrote so quickly, and she understood it all. So, one day we were in class and taking notes about what we were being taught; I thought I was clever, using this code to write notes. How fast my pencil flew across the paper – I was writing! I was really doing it!

And then Mr Gammon happened to look over my shoulder. He saw the nonsense scribbles I was 'writing' in my workbook and was furious. He didn't understand why I was doing it, and he didn't care. He grabbed my shoulder, ripping the sleeve from my shirt. I was doubly terrified then, not only of the beating I assumed I'd get at school but also because I knew how angry Dad would be about the ruined shirt. No one listened to my explanation. No one cared. And sure enough, when I got home, and Dad saw what had happened, he took his belt to me. The injustice of it still hurts when I think back, and I so wish I could have had a very different childhood.

There was one golden highlight of junior school, though, and as in all things ever since, I have learned to focus on the positives. At junior school, I learned to swim. Finally, here was something I could do and do well. I loved being in the water. I loved the sense of freedom it gave me. My legs didn't feel weak when I was in the pool – they propelled me through it just like all the other children. No one could get to me in the pool. It was the closest thing I had to a happy place. It was my haven, and I have loved the water ever since.

It takes an awful lot of resilience to ignore years of bullying and being singled out as stupid by adults and children alike. Getting beaten up on the way home from school and then being told off and belted at home for damaging my school uniform. The resilience that I just didn't have in those days; resilience that children often don't or can't have. So, I started to give up. What was the point in trying? I'd only fail and be punished, so I stopped even trying in the first place. The bullying continued into senior school, which was Frances Coombe School. Always compared, and unfavourably so, with Sandy and Susan's abilities, I was still considered the dunce of the family, a disappointment to everyone. I was in the lowest sets for everything, and I'd given up even trying to understand the school system.

Gradually I began to simply avoid people. I became a loner, both at school and at home. It was easy, and I was already having a lot of time off school for all my hospital visits – St Mary's for my allergies, St Thomas' for the bleeding from my kidneys which had started in earnest at 13, and Watford General for my legs. In the second year, the school finally took notice of how badly behind I was and gave me extra support with reading, but my attendance was so limited by then that it had little effect.

I made some bad decisions at senior school, which I can't defend really. I was so envious of the lives the other children had. I remember being so angry that we couldn't even afford the materials I needed for the model making classes. I couldn't ask Mum for the money; I knew we couldn't afford it, and I didn't want to make her feel bad. For the first couple of classes, I just made something up, said I'd forgotten to bring it, which I doubt the teacher ever believed. The other boys certainly didn't, and they teased me no end for being so poor. At the shops, I had all this anger seething through my head, and the models were just there, right there on the shelf. And I did something stupid. I stole one. And of course, because I'm me, I got caught – and believe me, I paid more than the price of the model when I got home. Not that I cared a lot by then – I was used to being a disappointment, and I was used to being punished for it. I was resigned to it by then, accepting of the fact that clearly, I was a failure in the eyes of the world.

I don't remember exactly when I left school, but I was only about 14 when I did. There are plenty of complaints about today's education system, I know, but I just hope that no young boy is ever made to feel the way I was, that no one is ever failed again by education as I felt I was back then.

This time has directly affected the way I handled things throughout my entire life. In some ways, I expect to fail at whatever I do. When I talk to people, I expect to get the worst outcome and feel that my point of view does not have any weight, that my opinion does not count, regardless of any evidence that shows me to be right. I still feel I'm the one doing wrong.

Mum, Dad and Grandmother in happy times, the 1960s

Chapter Two
Adventures and Repercussions

Of course, it wasn't all bad. I have some really happy memories of my childhood, mixed in with the bad stuff. Having that many children around all the time could be difficult, of course, and there were arguments and resentments aplenty. But there was a lot of fun too.

The children that Mum fostered ranged in age quite significantly, so there were always young ones who needed entertaining. Once I was 12 or 13, I was trusted to help out a bit, and I loved it. Maybe it was just a nice change of pace – having people looking up to me for a change, but whatever the reason, I really enjoyed looking after them.

I remember a time when Anne, one of my foster-sisters who was around the same age as me, and I decided to take the children out for a walk. We went further than we realised, out through Garston Park Woods, where we all loved playing. We had such a great time that day – covered from head to foot in mud and laughing our heads off. On the other side of the woods was a newly built road, which had been closed off to traffic while it was being built, so we had no idea it was open. So, there we were, playing on this massive road, with absolutely no idea that some helpful soul was busy reporting to the police that there was a bunch of children out playing on the M1!

We'd already headed home by the time the police got to the road to check on the reports. We were fine; it didn't occur to us that anyone might be worried or that we shouldn't have been playing where we were. We were totally oblivious when we got home – until we saw the police car.

Mum was furious. Not only had we been out for hours and been reported to the police, but we were also filthy. And our punishment still makes me cringe to this day – Anne and I were forced to take a bath together. At 13, that was totally mortifying and is still one of the punishments that I hated the most.

Before the M1 incident – I was about ten, I suppose – there was a period of time when I would go off with Sandy, who was four years older than me, to go horse-riding. Our local greengrocer had horses stabled at Bricket Wood, which he'd let us ride from time to time in exchange for mucking out and a few other yard jobs. It was a great arrangement from our perspective, and off we'd set every couple of weeks on the long walk. Although we both suffered from our breathing and skin for days afterwards, we believed at the time it was worth the pain because we were just having fun. This was one of the only things I did solely with Sandy, which made it all the better.

The stables were the other side of the wood, and we knew the road was a long way around, and of course, we were young, impatient and invincible. One day, we decided to take a shortcut and go straight through the woods. How hard could it be? We'd just go in a straight line and pop out the other side, saving probably an hour's walk. Genius, we thought.

So, in we went. Without the sun beating down, it was cool and shady in the woods, but as we walked, the trees became denser, the path withering to nothing much at all until we had no idea which direction we were walking in. All our Boys' Brigade knowledge of north-growing moss and following a compass (that we hadn't thought to bring) went out of the proverbial window, as the wind made strange noises in the darkening trees and our young imaginations went wild with fearful anticipation. We were spooked – good and proper – and we were also completely lost. I have no idea how long we stumbled around in there, the first flutters of worry turning to full-blown panic as trail after trail failed to provide us with an exit, and the woods stretched on before us, strange and dark and threatening.

After what felt like hours, we finally emerged into the sunshine again, triumphant that we had conquered the wood. But then we looked again, and realised we were in almost the same spot we had entered! Heads hanging, we got to the stables about three hours later than planned, and we vowed we'd never try that shortcut again.

That must have been a Saturday because every Sunday was dominated by two things: church and visiting Dad's mum, our grandma. Dad's brother, Uncle Jim, would come along with his children too, and it was always a riot catching up with the cousins. Grandma had a garden that felt like it stretched on forever, as a child, with different areas and a fruit patch at the bottom. Uncle Jimmy would come outside and play with us all, flinging us up in the air and catching us at the last minute. We loved it – all except for Susan, who hated being picked up. So, one day she decided she'd had enough of it, and as he went to pick her up, she bent down so he couldn't grab onto her. Unfortunately, she stood up at just the wrong moment and with a resounding crack, her head smashed into Uncle Jimmy's nose! Oh wow, I've never seen blood like it, gushing out and all over the place. We all thought it was absolutely hilarious, of course – there he was, big, tough Uncle Jimmy, taken out by a little girl! I doubt he found having his nose broken quite so funny, but the memory of it still makes me chuckle today.

Injuries were nothing new to me, of course. If there was an accident to be had, you could almost guarantee I'd be the one having it. Sometimes, when we were away camping, we'd go off fishing, hunting the little minnows in the river and trying to catch them in our nets. One time we were staying in Denham, near Uxbridge, and had walked a good three miles or so from the campsite to find a river to fish in. Before we left, Mum gave us strict instructions: Do not, under any circumstances, go into the river with your shoes on. I suspect the instruction also included something about 'or with them off', but I certainly didn't hear that bit. So, as usual, following rules to the letter – or so I thought, I took my shoes off and went into the river to fish.

What I didn't see was the broken bottles and glass that lined the riverbed – and by the time I realised they were there, it was too late. Now, when it comes to blood, I've always been very good at dealing with it – as long as it's someone else's. When it comes to my own, unfortunately, I'm not quite as stoic. So, when I saw the blood spurting out of my foot, I did what any helpful young lad would do – I passed out, leaving Susan to pick up the pieces. When I came around, my foot was bound and was stinging like anything. I ended up with five stitches in the sole of my foot, a furious sister who had been left to deal with not only my injury but all the younger children we had with us, and an even more irate mother, fuming that once again I'd ignored her explicit instructions. She didn't seem to hear when I said that at least I'd taken my shoes off.

One thing I really enjoyed was my time in the Boys' Brigade through the church. There were three of us, great friends, who went along and all had a huge interest in motorbikes and scooters. We managed to get our hands on two Lambretta scooters and a Honda 125 twin and fixed them up ourselves, teaching ourselves about engines in the process. One of the dads was happy for us to keep the bikes in his garage, and once we'd got them up and running, we'd take them out racing around the local fields. I even used to ride the motorbike to school sometimes. I used to stash it in a friend's garden and naively thought my mum knew nothing about it – how wrong I was, but at the time, I thought I was getting away with it completely.

But although those incidents, like so many in my life, so often ended up with me in a heap of uninvited trouble or getting injured, they were great days, and there were a lot of them. Carefree day of play and sunshine, all those many, many children who have gone on to lead such varied lives, oblivious to the responsibilities and heartbreaks still to come. I like to think we appreciated what we had back then – and the memories still bring me happiness amongst the challenges.

Mum's side of our family.

My brother's wedding 1978, As you can see we are starting to see Grandchildren now.

Chapter Three
Everything Changed

It was pretty obvious to me and to those around me that school wasn't for me. Unhappy, lonely and failing to learn anything, by the time I was 14, my dad had had enough. "Enough time-wasting," he said. "It's time you got a job."

I had no idea that those words would be among the most life-changing I'd ever hear.

Unbeknownst to me, he'd had a word with the manager at Bushey Vale Garage and got me a position there as a workshop assistant. I'd harboured dreams of becoming a carpenter, but my dad's response was that I was to get a 'real job', and as he'd sorted it out for me, I couldn't very well say no. It may not have been my dream job, but for the first time, my dad had shown an interest in me, and I was feeling more positive than I could ever remember feeling.

And so, on 3rd July 1972 – 18 days before my 15th birthday – I started work. At that point, I really was a general dogsbody, sweeping floors, making the tea, fetching and carrying– whatever anyone needed me to do, really. And that was fine. Not being at school, being in the workplace, being around cars – this was the happiest I'd been for a long time.

I hid my issues as best I could, hoping no one would notice that I still couldn't read. I should have known better.

My service manager, John Briggs, was more observant than I had realised. What I didn't know at that time was that he had a young son who also struggled with reading and writing. But where I had been punished and made to feel like an idiot, his son was getting help. One day, Mr Briggs called me into his office, asking me to bring with me some particular paperwork. Unable to read the details, I grabbed what I thought was the right set and hoped for the best. A woman was sitting in his office when I went in, who he introduced to me as Mrs Wolf. This was to be one of the most significant days of my life. Mrs Wolf was the teacher helping Mr Briggs' son to read, and she had some experience of a condition called dyslexia. Of course, I'd never heard of it, but for the first time, here was an explanation of why I struggled so much to make sense of words when I saw them written down. I wasn't stupid – I was dyslexic. It had a name. And if it had a name, maybe, just maybe, it had a cure. Hope flared.

For the next six months, I had lessons with Mrs Wolf. I'd never had a reason to try before, but now that I understood why I found it so hard, I found it easier to try. I made good progress, and it had an effect on every area of my life. Even my hospital visits reduced drastically, and I began to really enjoy the job and my life for the first time. I had friends, a girlfriend, Rosemary, a caretaker's daughter from church… things were going great. I was worried when the school got in touch to demand I go back, as I'd left before I was 15, but my manager was so pleased with my work that he took me on as an apprentice, meaning I didn't have to go back to school. It was a new beginning, and I was discovering what it was like to be happy.

I should have known it was too good to last. In September 1973, everything changed.

I was cycling to work one morning. I like to think I was thinking positively about the day ahead and counting my blessings, though I suspect my thoughts were a lot less relevant than that. So, there I was, cycling along, when a Ford Anglia (I remember that part vividly) pulled out of a side road, straight into my path. I was hit by the car's offside front wing with such force that I was thrown up in the air, right over a single-decker bus and crashed down on the bonnet of a Rover 90. I rolled off and struck the ground, splitting my head open. The next thing I knew, I was back in the hospital again.

118 stitches. Yes, 118 stitches to piece my head back together, and I still have the scar today. I was kept in hospital for some time, so of course, I couldn't work and naturally, everything began to go downhill. The accident seemed to have opened the floodgates on my health, which had seemed so much better for the preceding months, and my time in the hospital began to creep up again. I was bleeding badly from my kidneys still, which the doctors were concerned about but never were able to find a reason for. They gave me test after invasive test, trying this and that and the other, but never giving me any answers and never listening when I told them about new symptoms. I had pain in other organs too, but despite my medical history, everyone insisted on treating me like I was being a hypochondriac.

Another blow was struck when my girlfriend left me. She delivered the bombshell that she was pregnant – which was a particular surprise to me since I was still reeling from the news from one of my doctors that I would never be able to father children. At the age I was then, I probably wasn't as bothered as I would have been later, but it was still a shock and something I was still struggling to come to terms with when my girlfriend gave me her news. As it turned out, she wasn't pregnant at all, but the break-up was another assault on my self-esteem, and I was feeling pretty bleak again.

During 1974, I spent a lot of time in hospital with one illness or another. The bleeding from my kidneys was getting worse, as was the pain in my other organs. Work was good to me, putting me on light duties whenever I was able to be there at all and eventually, they moved me into the office and storefront rather than the garage itself, so I didn't have to be so physical. But my health continued to deteriorate. My weight fluctuated wildly; due to excessive fluid retention, I ballooned to 18 stone, dropping to just 6½ stone only weeks later after another stint in hospital. In September, I was dealt another blow: my parents split up. I'd been in the hospital for some time just before they announced the break-up, and I honestly did feel responsible. I knew I'd been a burden, a disappointment, and I could only assume that finally, the pressure of having me had been too much.

Sometime before this, my dad had been made redundant from Odhams, the print company he'd worked at for over 20 years. Needing income, he took a job in sales. They gave him a car, a red Mark 3 Ford Cortina, and he was on the road for weeks at a time, only returning home at weekends and sometimes not even then. His patch was around Bristol, the other side of the country to us. His time away grew longer and longer, sometimes up to a month at a time. I suppose, looking back, it should have been obvious that something was going on, that he had other reasons to stay away, but it didn't really occur to me at the time. Even when I realised they weren't happy, I never thought they'd actually break up – they were Mum and Dad, they were a fact– a unit. They would be together forever.

So, when I was rushed into the hospital to have some more investigative work done, following more internal bleeding and now with some bladder issues added to the mix, it wasn't Dad who came with Mum to see me. I'd been down for an operation, and I was coming around from that when my mum appeared with her friend, who we all referred to as Auntie Margaret. Of course, I'd expected Dad to be there; this was at a time when the doctors were trying to explain to me that these health issues I was suffering from were actually life-threatening, so I'd been hoping they'd come in together.

"We're getting divorced," she said. "He's moved out. You'll have to put up with me visiting you on my own." I remember the look on her face when she said it. It was almost a relief, after the years of arguments and how Dad had treated us on occasion. Maybe Mum would be happier. But it really hit home and set the tone for the rest of my life. If you commit to something, you should commit wholeheartedly; you shouldn't ever give up, just ditch your responsibilities and run away.

Mum's visits became further apart because even in those days, it was nearly a two-hour journey from Garston to The Embankment, London. Now I had to get used to seeing someone no more than once a week. I never saw my brothers or sister during this time either. I was alone again.

They never explained what happened, not really – I've pieced it together for myself in the years since, and I wouldn't have expected a straight answer anyway. While my childhood had not been the happiest, their relationship had always been a solid feature of it, the foundation for our enormous, unusual family. Everything was unravelling, and I was convinced that I was to blame.

I wanted to get them back together again; I realise how naïve that may seem now, but really, I was still a child, without any real understanding of grown-up relationships. And, of course, divorce was not so common back then. I thought if I could fix this, then I could do anything. I desperately tried to get them talking. But I realise now it was a very bitter divorce; with so many children involved and so much going on with all of us, how could it not be. Sandy was away in the navy at that time, and Sue was in the TAs, and I felt it was down to me. But because of my health and work, I hadn't been there to mediate, and of course, I felt sure that it was partly the pressures I put on them with my health and behaviour that led to their break-up. I've never really been able to shake off that feeling. Right up to the day he died, I kept on trying to get them talking again, but he wasn't really interested in us. I missed him dreadfully, despite how he'd treated us at times. It's strange how we cling to what we know, even if it isn't necessarily good for us.

But back then, lying in that hospital bed, it came as a hefty blow. My whole world was collapsing, and I was helpless to prevent it. Mum carried on with the fostering and never confided in us about how hard any of it was, but the strain must have been enormous. In November 1974, things came to a head. I'd been having dialysis for my kidneys and was taking a complex cocktail of drugs for the pain and my other conditions. And hard as that was, it never really occurred to me that it might not last. So, when Dr Norman Jones sat me down and explained that, despite all their best efforts, no more could be done, I didn't really understand what he was saying. No more treatments? No more options?

I was 16 years old.

However hard my life had been, and however frequent my medical emergencies, the idea that I might reach a stage where the doctors could do nothing had not really occurred to me. I couldn't process it at all at first; back then, there wasn't a standard process of psychiatric support, so there was no one to help me deal with it, or make plans, or come to terms with my prognosis. My whole world had collapsed, and all I wanted to do was turn the lights off. I didn't suspect for a moment that everything was about to change yet again – nor that this time, it would be for the better.

Chapter Four
New Beginnings

I wasn't in a great place at that point and got into some stupid situations, some of which have had a big impact on me ever since. There was a time, just after I'd come out of the hospital, when some mates decided to try to cheer me up and took me out. We went to the Green Man pub in Watford, had a few beers (I don't think people checked IDs quite as much back then – we were only 16 yet had no issues getting served) and ended up wandering around a multi-storey car park late at night. I'm still not quite sure how it happened, but we all ended up getting into this mini that was parked there, the engine roared into life, and off we went. I don't think it really occurred to me that we were stealing it – not really. Until the police caught up with us, that is. Being arrested was an eye-opening experience. I was charged with aiding and abetting theft. In the end, it took so long to get to court (around three years, in fact) that I was actually legally an adult by the time it did. That ended up working in my favour as I was being tried as an adult – until, of course, the defence solicitor pointed out that I had been a minor at the time, and the charges ended up being thrown out. A fortunate clerical error that saved me from having a permanent black mark against me on my record. I've been arrested a couple of times since – as you'll discover later on – but that first time was the most formative, the only time I had honestly done something wrong, and it really made me take stock of my life and realise that I didn't want to be that person. I've always tried to respect others and be law-abiding. Sometimes circumstances have conspired against me, but I have a healthy respect for the law – if not always for those employed to uphold it.

After that, things went downhill. I stopped accepting invitations from friends to go out and sank into depression. My friends were getting pretty fed up with me. I never wanted to go out anywhere, so if they wanted to see me, they ended up having to just sit around in the lounge at my house, surrounded by my family. Not really anyone's idea of a good time, but I couldn't face leaving the house most of the time. I was becoming more and more reclusive, even starting to turn down the offer of visits and just wanting to withdraw from everyone and everything.

But on 3rd January 1975, those mates finally had enough. "You're coming out with us," they said. They were due to go off on holiday together soon afterwards, so I knew I wouldn't see them again for ages. If I'd had more time to argue, I probably wouldn't have gone, but they literally gave me 15 minutes and were prepared to drag me out kicking and screaming. Left with little choice, I got myself together and went. I'd not been looking after myself well at that point, having given up on just about everything. I'd wasted away to just 6½ stone, which at my height 5' 10" was quite a dramatic look, and I just had no energy for anything.

Off we went to Baileys Nightclub in Watford. I had no idea that this would be one of the most fateful nights of my life.

My friends were all off, chatting up girls and creating havoc. I stood at the upstairs bar, nursing a glass of orange and wishing I hadn't come out.

"Excuse me," said a voice. "Do you have change for a five-pound note?"

I looked around, and there was a girl standing in front of me. "Oh – um," I said. To think, I was only earning £8 a week as an apprentice, and she was asking for change for a fiver! I fished around in my pocket, knowing it was futile, and could only come up with a 20 pence piece. "That's not really enough." We laughed.

"I'm Jan," she said. And that was it. Janet Susan Violet. The one true love of my life.

We spent the whole of that first evening together, talking and laughing, much to the amusement of my friends. It was only, later on, I learned that, like me, Jan had been strong-armed into being there that night by her own friends, so in fact, neither of us had planned or even wanted to be there in the first place. But there we were, and I felt like I could talk to her forever.

At the end of the evening, we exchanged phone numbers and addresses and made arrangements to meet up a couple of weeks later. I didn't really believe she'd go through with it, this lovely girl who had come out of nowhere and woken me up. The feeling of that first meeting stayed with me, and I just couldn't get her out of my head. I was so sure that she wouldn't go through with our arranged rendezvous that I worked myself up into a frenzy of impatience. I just couldn't wait two weeks!

Jan off on her last holiday with her parents, July 1975.

So, throwing caution to the wind, I turned up at her door a week early and completely unannounced. The door was opened by an older man, who I learned to be Jan's father, Reg. I introduced myself, and he called up the stairs, which were right in front of the front door, giving me a perfect view. I looked up; Jan emerged and absolutely took my breath away.

This was not the girl I remembered from the bar – this was a stunning, beautiful woman, dressed in a full-length red polka dot halter-neck dress. She was more gorgeous than I had remembered, more grown-up and more lovely. I literally couldn't speak.

Jan explained that she was getting ready to go to a family party in Luton, organised by her brother-in-law, Terry, and she introduced me to her family. I shook hands dutifully, unable to take my eyes off Jan the whole time. And then she awkwardly pointed out that I was a week early.

Jan and her mum and dad.

I'd been given a lift by my mum, so the family minibus was parked outside, full to bursting with my family, all waiting with great interest to see who it was I was meeting up with. I said I'd leave, that we could meet up the next week as planned and was just about to go when Terry stepped forward and suggested I went along to the party – there was room in their car, he said, so why not?

It was a big step and a very quick way to get to know her family. I wasn't sure if she wanted me there or not, and I was nervous about returning to Luton, where, on my last visit, I'd been beaten up and ended up in hospital. But this was an opportunity not to be missed, and I was sure that with Jan by my side, it would be a great evening. So, I agreed and told my mum I'd be back late. With a great sense of trepidation and apprehension, I plunged into the evening and a whole new life.

We had a wonderful time that evening. We talked and talked and laughed, and I got to know Jan and her family well. This was an intelligent, independent woman with ambition and plans for herself. I could tell that, as the youngest, her parents were very protective. I suppose they only ever wanted the very best for their daughter, and I'm not sure I ever really matched their expectations. Perhaps no man would ever have been good enough for their little girl – but Jan was no little girl by this time, and she was not likely to listen to anyone else having a say in her life. Of course, I had very little money in those days. I was still an apprentice at the garage, going to college two days every week, so funds were pretty tight. However, we made every effort to meet up as much as possible, usually about once a fortnight. We'd catch the last bus back to Jan's after our dates, and then I'd walk the 12 or so miles back to Garston. You can't imagine how long it took me, given the state of my legs, but I was happy to do it, as it meant I got longer with Jan. One night– still at just seven stone and feeling exhausted– a speeding lorry passed me and created such a draft that it knocked me right off my feet!

As we got to know each other better, I had to share my medical troubles with Jan. It was such a big part of my life there was no way to keep it secret, and she was so supportive. She started coming with me to some of my regular hospital appointments, wanting to hear first-hand what the doctors were saying and to share her own observations of my various conditions. She had seen me being rushed into hospital on more than one occasion, even just in those first few weeks, so I knew she wasn't, at all, phased by it all. I asked her to come with me to see a consultant. And so, on Tuesday 4th March 1975, off we went. I remember the date so clearly and even the time. It was 2:40 pm when he gave me the news. There we were, all poised with our questions about my future – questions like "will I be able to father a child?" despite having been told before that I couldn't; questions about my treatment and how I could manage as well possible. But at 2:40 pm, all that changed. The consultant, Dr Norman Jones, explained to me that there was simply nothing more that could be done. By his estimate, I had no more than two years to live.

I was almost back at square one, trying to process what I had been told and come to terms with my short life expectancy. Almost, but not quite. Because I had Jan, we spent a lot of time together over the next few days, and she listened, and she spoke, and she understood. I was – and still am – so grateful that she was there with me through that. And so it was that on 8th March, just four days after I'd been told I was going to die, on the day of Jan's 18th birthday, I went to her mum and dad's house, and I asked her to marry me.

Jan's 18th birthday, March 1975 – the day I proposed.

Chapter Five
The Greatest Day

I think most people have a preconceived notion of what a marriage proposal should be like. Some have wishes and dreams; some have it all mapped out. I didn't, not really. But I knew I loved Jan with all my heart, and I knew I wanted to marry her. I knew she didn't feel the same way, although we were such good friends, and I knew she cared about me.

My proposal certainly took her by surprise. She gaped at me and blurted out, "But I don't love you!" "You will," I said with absolute certainty. "And I most certainly love you." She took some persuading since she was concerned – yes, she cared deeply for me, but she didn't feel she had fallen in love. However, the more we talked, and I reminded her somewhat wryly that it would only be for a couple of years, she agreed. It might not be everyone's idea of a perfect start to a marriage, but ours has outlasted most that I know of, and she has made me a very happy man. I could not foresee then all the ups and downs in the road ahead of us, but I knew wholeheartedly that I loved her, and there was no one else I wanted by my side.

We started planning the wedding and set a date of 15th November 1975. I don't think the date had any particular significance – it was probably just the first date we were given by the church and the hall, and we took it. Soon after that, I moved into a bedsit in Church Lane in Mill End so I could be closer to her. I also needed to reduce the amount of walking I had to do – my legs were getting weaker, and my health was deteriorating. I lost my apprenticeship not long after I moved because of the amount of time I had to take off for hospital appointments and general sickness.

But strangely, once I stopped worrying about the short timescale and just got on with the planning and my everyday life, things actually started to get better. I wanted to make the most of what little time I had left, and my positive attitude had benefits to my health, as I started having longer and longer gaps between bouts of illness. I have no doubt that it was Jan who kick-started the positive thinking, and I don't think I'd realised until that point what a positive influence she was. I needed to get back to work, and I found a job at the nearby Dairy Express as a yardman, which helped me get back on my feet. That July, I turned 18, and they offered me a job as a milkman, which I took as I needed the pay raise it offered. The job was very physical, and it took me longer to do my round than the others, but it gave me another reason to get out of bed in the mornings.

I found the work immensely rewarding, which surprised me. I was working to meet other people's needs, and I started to find that I could help them in other ways – like collecting their shopping for them and dropping it off along with their milk. I found a flat above one of the shops I delivered to and secured a decent rent. I moved in during October – finally, Jan and I would have somewhere to call home once we were married.

Time was passing quickly, and the date of the wedding was drawing nearer. Two days before the wedding, I went around to Jan's house to have a chat – but true to form, accident-prone Andy was alive and well, and I managed to split my head open on the overhang above the stairs! Another rushed trip to the hospital, and four stitches later, I was all patched up. I'd have to brush my hair to one side to hide the injury for the wedding photographs, that was for sure! Fortunately, there were no complications, and the wedding could proceed. Even at that point, Jan wasn't able to tell me she loved me – but what the hell? We were both happy to be getting married, and it was the start of a great adventure. The day arrived at last; I was nervous but excited. My brother Sandy was my best man, and in a true style, he stayed at my flat the night before, and en route to the church, being driven by my dad, we stopped at all the pubs along the way! We limited it to one drink in each (and I didn't drink alcohol, so the effects were non-existent), but it was great fun. We got to the church on time, and I stood, looking at the damp but sunny autumn day and felt so happy that this was happening.

Jan arrived at last, with her sisters, Pat (as matron of honour) and Amanda (as a bridesmaid). I'll never forget how she looked that day, as she became my wife.

Jan and I signing the register, 15 November 1975.

It was a day to be remembered by all who attended and one of the happiest of my life.

We hadn't arranged to have a honeymoon away, which was fortunate as I had an appointment three days later at the hospital to have my stitches removed. We had booked a couple of nights at the Noke Hotel in St Albans, though, and it was a wonderful surprise on arrival to be told we'd been upgraded to the bridal suite. What a perfect end to a perfect day. Once the stitches were out, we spent another happy few days at Southend, enjoying the pier and the wonderful winter views of the sea.

More than forty years have passed since that momentous day, and every day I am grateful that it happened. Jan has been my partner through a lot of hardships and a lot of ups and downs, and it hasn't always been easy. But we make a good team, and I knew that from the start. She was the girl for me from the minute I met her, and she still is today.

Some of my extended family.

Jan and I with our parents, my brother Sandy, and Jan's bridesmaids – her sister Pat and niece Amanda.

Chapter Six
An Unexpected Family

In those early days after the wedding, we were working as a team, building both a home and a life together. After the wedding and our few days away – two of which we spent under the pier at Southend as I could not afford a room – we returned to work, me as a milkman and Jan to her job as a clerk at Three Rivers CC.

I enjoyed the job, and in the weeks leading up to Christmas, I was really making an extra effort to get as many tips as possible. I liked making others' lives easier, collecting groceries and so on, as well as delivering those that we milkmen delivered as part of our rounds; quite a few of the people on my rounds were elderly, and I felt that I was really able to make a difference to them by collecting extra bits and bobs for them as well as the things they bought through the dairy. I was looking forward to a Christmas bonus roughly equivalent to another month's wages, thanks to customer tips.

However, one week my milk bag came up short, and in the heat of the moment, I just couldn't account for the shortfall. Of course, I realised later; I'd used some of the milk money floats to pay for the extra groceries for a couple of people; ordinarily, that would be paid straight back in when I delivered it, and they paid me back, but that week, two of them had been short of cash. But those details left me when I was confronted about it. I made money up out of my own cash – I even had to speak to Jan about it since without my wages for that month, we'd be short on rent, so had to use hers to pay it. What I didn't realise was that my conversation was overheard by the foreman, who, without waiting for my explanation, assumed I was hard up and had embezzled the money to pay my rent. I was sacked without pay – and I'd learnt a very valuable life lesson about careful accounting, and about other people's tendencies to judge without waiting for the facts.

Two weeks until Christmas, and I had not only missed out on my bonus (the foreman had benefited from that to the tune of around £700) but was now unemployed. It was a pretty shaky start to our marriage and put a huge amount of strain on our relationship. It also gave me the insight to realise that every penny needs to be accounted for and has made me scrupulously conscientious about keeping absolutely accurate records ever since, which has stood me in good stead running any kind of business, especially my own, to this very day.

Not one to give up easily, I looked around for more work and was very focussed on proving to people that I could do it– that I would provide for my wife. I soon found work as a motor mechanic, though I'm not proud to admit that I got the job by pretending I had qualifications that I simply didn't possess. But I could do the job well, and the level of work suited me, so no one discovered my deception – but as usual, it wasn't long before my health got in the way.

Working in such cold conditions, my kidneys started to play up again and I was taken very ill. The upshot of that was to lose the job – and this was a pattern that continued for the next year, getting myself a new job only to be taken ill and laid off again. However, one positive at that time was that despite all the bouts of illness, I was able to get my qualification as an MOT tester, which made talking my way into new jobs much easier, and I even spent some time working as a roadside assistance mechanic on 24-hour call-out.

I was well aware by this time that my two years of predicted life was rapidly running out. My health was unreliable and I didn't know how accurate the doctor's timescale was, but the day of reckoning came and went, and I simply kept going, one day after another, never knowing whether I'd be alive at the end of each week or not.

All the different jobs I'd had in this period had taught me a lot about applying for and getting employment, and I always seemed to find a new job when another one ended. However, the long, physical days were taking their toll and I knew I couldn't keep up with the work for long. It was at that point I made the decision to try management and I got a job as a manager at High Street Service Station, Watford; responsible for running the workshop and the 24-hour roadside assistance service. I was office-based most of the time, which made things easier on me physically and I was enjoying the work. And then another bombshell hit: Jan announced that she was pregnant.

My first reaction was rather unfavourable: I assumed she had been having an affair and was pregnant by another man. After all, the doctors had told me I couldn't have children (though I'm not sure Jan was fully aware of that at the time!), and I'd been working long hours at the garage and not been at home as much as I would have liked. But then it occurred to me that I shouldn't even be there at all according to the doctors, and if they'd got something as monumental as life and death wrong, then perhaps they'd misjudged this too.

On Jan's birthday, 8th March 1979, I received a phone call at work asking me to go to my mum's house, 23 Garston Lane, as there had been a tragedy. I arrived to find my brother, Victor, had taken his own life. He was just 16 years old.

Victor had been accused of assaulting a young girl in Garston Park and spent six hours being quizzed by Watford Police before being released. As a family, we knew that Victor was not guilty. He was a self-confessed homosexual. Within a couple of hours of hearing news of Victor's death, the young girl admitted to a false accusation. Victor had shunned her advances and she wanted to get back at him, get him into trouble. His name was cleared of any wrongdoing.

Jan's pregnancy continued reasonably smoothly apart from Jan suffering toxaemia and me having a 'run in' with one of her doctors at Watford General Hospital. As a result, Jan switched to the care of High Wycombe Hospital. I had been racing all day at Bovingdon oval circuit. I still had the panda face from the googles and I was just getting into the shower when Jan yelled out "something has happened." There was a pool of water on our new bedroom carpet. She was holding her night gown up and looking at the floor. As this was our first experience of childbirth, we did not know what to do, other than call the hospital. I was told to get her to the hospital ASAP.

Banger racing crash!

This I did, from Maple Cross to High Wycombe in 22 minutes. I was told to go home as, "it will be hours yet, get washed and changed before you come back," they said. So, back home, I got in the shower, soaped up and the phone rang. "Can you get back, we are taking your wife down to the delivery room? How long will it take you?" I just said, "I will get there as quick as I can." It was a long and worrying night of labour and birth, but we were delighted to welcome our son Russell into the world at 4:00 am on 28th August 1979. With Jan giving up her job to focus on Russell, money was now very tight and it was up to me to provide for my growing family. I was on the lookout for better work, but it's hard to think long term when you've got a death sentence hanging over your head. I was bleeding internally again, and the doctors were still saying nothing could be done.

I found I could make better money as a motor mechanic than as a manager at that point, so that's what I did, and continued to do for the next two years as Russell took his first steps, learned his first words and gave us both a lot of very happy memories.

Two years later, on 27th November 1981, we had another unexpected blessing: our daughter.

The year before Emma came into this world, I spent as much time as I could with Russell, 1980.

Jan and baby Russell.

With Jan and Russell...

New-born Emma.

A few months after Emma was born, we had a stroke of good luck when the local council moved us from a top floor flat into a three-bedroom house. We felt like royalty! It was such a luxury to have the extra space and we were overjoyed with our new place. However, after a couple of months, both Russell and I started to get ill, and it transpired that the house was riddled with bugs. The council reluctantly agreed that something had to be done and that they would deal with the infestations if we moved out while they did it. Of course, we couldn't afford to stay somewhere else, but we were able to borrow a caravan and parked it out in the front garden.

Disaster struck again as we were moving things out of the house; I slipped and broke my ankle. I had to have a plaster cast, so there we were, coming into winter, living in a caravan in our front garden with me in plaster and two young children to look after. Emma was just over a year old by then but still had no hair at all because she'd developed a severe cradle cap. It did start to come through a few months later though, we were relieved to see. We had a fraught few weeks in that caravan, but in December we were able to move back into our house, just in time for Christmas. No one could say that the early years of our children's lives were the smoothest, but we carried on regardless, getting used to family life, and enjoying our bug-free house. After a long talk with the council about the house and the troubles we'd had, they agreed to move us back to Maple Cross, at 33 Horn Hill Road, which they had just finished refurbishing. It was like moving into a brand-new house after the state of the last one! Things settled for a while and we were able to just get on with life. Even the uncertainty of my health didn't seem to be looming so badly at that stage, and we were able to enjoy our little family.

I lost another job not long afterwards but found another which meant I had to travel daily to Edgware Road in London. It was a long way but the positive was that I was given a work car, so it was manageable. All in all, it wasn't a bad time in our lives. Really, I should have known things were about to get a whole lot worse. I didn't – but it wasn't long before they did. But before I go into all that, there's a whole other chapter of my life that had been going on alongside all this that I have barely touched on but can't leave out.

Some family photos from the children's early years

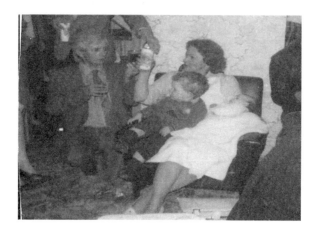

Emma's Christening, Emma's second Christmas, 1982.

Russell and Emma get a taste of mechanics, 1984

Chapter Seven
The Thrill of the Race

Being told you have only two years to live has quite an effect. I was already on a high from the wedding, from embarking on this huge adventure with Jan, but of course, I had this death sentence hanging over me. Our marriage had made me so happy, and I was determined to fill what time I had left with as much happiness and excitement as possible – to live whatever life I had left to the full.

Showing my skills on the water.

I had always had a real passion for motor racing. I'd never given it a go – with my track record of accidents, it had never seemed like a good idea. But somehow now, I felt both – that I had nothing much to lose and that I was running out of time to try the things I'd always wanted to try.

Hot Rod & Russell first visit to the track.

Suddenly the dangers of racing cars didn't seem so bad – after all, I was dying anyway, so I might as well enjoy myself.

The crowd at the races.

That's how it started. Banger racing back in the late '70s, probably the most dangerous option available. And I can honestly say, from the moment I started, I absolutely loved it. I knew all about cars of course and had spent plenty of time putting engines together over the years. But now it was my turn to drive, and the thrill of it was immense.

Despite my accident-prone nature, I actually made an effort to steer clear of the crashes in racing, and it worked well – I was good. In one season between March and October, I went from a white top novice to a gold top. This was new, being good at something, being recognised for being good at it, for progressing. My health wasn't holding me back when I was behind the wheel, and the whole thing was incredibly liberating. Jan enjoyed it too and would come along and watch. Once I was at the top of the circuit, of course, I wanted to go further, and then got into racing hot rods, again going from white top novice to chequer top in my first season. I started off as a novice in Bovingdon, but within a year or so I was touring the country, racing all over the place. Jan was so supportive and came along to watch, witnessing some pretty serious accidents – but we loved it. Life was good.

Of course, doing things properly and on a national scale didn't come cheap. Maybe it was a reckless way to live, not just the driving but the high costs too, but I had two years left, or so I thought. I was on borrowed time. So, spending nearly £20K a year, which was a LOT of money back then, for three seasons, was a huge investment. Even when Russell came along in 1979, I kept going for another season. But things were changing. For a start, my two years were up and yet here I still was. The cost was racking up, and now we had a baby to think about too. My perspective was changing and we decided between us that we simply couldn't maintain that lifestyle. The expense and the risks were just too high now we had Russell to think about. I packed it all in, but it has always remained a passion of mine. I retained my licence until just a few years ago and dabbled in saloon car racing (now known as touring car racing) and have built plenty of cars for other people for racing, but from that time it had to take a back seat.

Banger racing.

Russell and Emma always showed an interest in cars and car racing too. Not long after we started at Andy's Kars (more about Andy's Kars later), they really wanted to give it a try, so we built a lightning rod for them and they absolutely loved it. But Jan and I knew the cost of taking it seriously, the commitment and time required, and with a young family and a budding business, we knew it wouldn't be something we could take on in any serious way.

I will always look back fondly on those days of racing; the thrill, the excitement, the rush of it all, the feeling that I just didn't care what happened. The feeling of winning, of Jan and me touring the country, me racing and her there in the crowd – it was an amazing time of our lives and one I'll always look back on with enormous happiness. And it's important, I think, to remember those happy times – because what happened next almost derailed everything.

Chapter Eight
A Turning Point

1983 started off with a headache. Or rather, it started with several. On 10th February, I was taken to Edgware Hospital. You've probably heard the expression 'blinding headache' but this one literally was. I couldn't see through the pain, but after three hours or so I was sent home with a suspected severe migraine. Headaches were a frequent event for me and usually, I just took a couple of Panadol and got on with it. It didn't really help, but the GP wouldn't listen and even told me I was being a hypochondriac. This was nothing new, of course, and by that time I was used to doctors not really listening to what I was telling them. So off I went and put up with the headaches – until the pain became so bad, I just couldn't function anymore.

The 16th June 1983 began as an ordinary day at the garage with several cars in for servicing and MOT's. We were not able to carry out MOT's ourselves, so they had to go across the road to another garage. It was about a five-minute walk back. On the way back from taking a vehicle there, I was crossing the Edgware Road, when it felt like I had been hit with a sledgehammer to my right temple. The last thing I can remember was a police van full of police officers passing by and I tried to hit the side to get their attention. That didn't work! Somehow, I managed to get back to the workshop where I collapsed fully. I do not remember the ambulance or arriving at the hospital. After six days in Edgware Hospital I was discharged, yet again being told I had a migraine. I had numbness all down my right arm, which the doctors still blamed on the 'migraine', and I was told to come back a week later. A week passed and I duly returned and finally saw a more senior doctor. Senior or not though, he still couldn't find a cause for the painful headaches, so he said I'd need to go to Maida Vale Hospital for a scan. Scans were fairly new at that point, so I had no idea what to expect, but I went along with the plan, desperate for something to alleviate the pain and resolve the numbness down my right side which was making me limp and fall over.

Three days later, Jan took me along for my appointment. By this point, I could barely stand up unassisted and the nurse who did my scan assumed I was an in-patient at the hospital – she was quite surprised after I'd had the scan when I informed her, I was going home! I wasn't really able to concentrate on what I was being told, so when she asked me to wait outside, I thought she was telling me I could go home. So, home we went.

The next morning, Jan took the children off to school as usual, and while she was out, the hospital called. They'd been looking for me, they said, they needed to see me urgently and would send an ambulance to pick me up. I really couldn't understand what they were talking about, but I agreed to go back to the hospital. I don't need an ambulance though, I told them, assuring them that Jan could bring me over once she was back from the school run. They could at least then explain to her what was going on since I wasn't really able to make sense of anything.

Within ten minutes of arriving at the hospital, they'd put me in a bed with strict instructions not to move. I had had a cerebral haemorrhage: my brain was bleeding. The brain bleed was the cause of the headaches, the cause of the numbness and loss of mobility down my right side. They needed to do more tests, they said, to find out why it had happened. Finally! I was to get some answers to what had been wrong with me all my life. I agreed, with pleasure, because I had always wanted to know the reasons for all my illnesses. It looked like that was finally going to happen, and I'd have agreed to just about anything at that point.

It was the worst decision of my life – and very nearly the one that ended it. In order to find out what was going on, the doctors needed to pump an iodine dye into my blood so they could monitor what was happening. But the dye put me into a coma, which I stayed in for six weeks. I saw the white light.

Of course, being in a coma, I don't remember much. However, I do have a vision of sitting on the curtain rail looking down at myself and watching as I was slipping away to the white light. Jan has filled me in where she can, though of course, she had to take care of the children too. But three days, in particular, stand out in her memory: the three times the hospital called to tell her I was dying.

The first time, she dropped everything and ran. By the third time, she finished cooking dinner and closed up the house properly before making her way over. The hospital had told her on each occasion that this would be her last chance to say goodbye, but she tells me to this day that she never really believed them – she said I was far too obstinate to leave her like that!

Jan's faith in my determination to stay alive turned out to be justified. Though it was a tough road getting there. I only found out afterwards that I had at one point been pronounced dead and wheeled off to the morgue. Fortunately, someone – someone whose name I will probably never know – spotted some tiny sign of life and realised a terrible mistake had been made.

Waking up was a traumatic experience. I had no idea where I was, and I discovered that I could neither see properly nor speak, and the whole right side of my body was paralysed. It was terrifying, and I became extremely agitated – yet I was powerless to communicate my fear, my thoughts, my horror at what was happening to me.

There were a lot of conversations going on around me. Perhaps no one realised that the one thing that was unaffected, was my hearing, or perhaps no one cared what I overheard. I'm not sure even I cared, for a while. I simply lay there, wondering why I had lived, wondering if this was all there was going to be for me. Unable to speak, see or move. Maybe I even stopped trying. And then one day, I overheard a conversation that was to change my life again: the doctor, speaking to Jan. And he said that I would never recover. He said I would be a "vegetable" – never able to look after myself, or walk, or speak.

Bugger that. No doctor had ever been right about me before, and I was damn sure this wasn't going to be the first. I was going to get better. My story was not over yet.

Chapter Nine
The Road to Recovery

I never realised quite how hard the path to recovery would be, nor how frustrating. I just couldn't do things that before I hadn't even had to think about. I couldn't pick things up, or speak properly, or get around. Every word was an effort, as was every movement. I seemed to talk through the side of my face and stammered a lot. Picking up a cup of water was almost impossible, and I would nearly always drop it. My movement improved but I could not walk unaided. I was often angry, depressed and frustrated.

Jan brought the children to see me as often as she could and I enjoyed playing with them. We would sit and do simple jigsaws, pictures and puzzles, and although they enjoyed our "play" time, this was invaluable therapy for me, teaching me from scratch, things I was no longer able to do. They helped me through this time much more than they ever knew, and although I may not always have said it, I was grateful to Jan for being there, and for bringing them. I made enormous progress from where I had been over the first two months, and I began to think about work. At that stage though, it was just that – a thought. I still had to concentrate hard to string even simple sentences together, and my coordination had a long way to go. For some reason, I was not given any physio once

I had come home, I was told a good few years later that my paperwork was lost in the transfer from Maida Vale to Mount Vernon. But after six months of trying to recover, I received a letter from my work: if I did not return to work within the next two weeks, my position would be terminated. I knew I would never find another job in my current condition, so I knew the only option was to try even harder. It was a kick in the ribs – but it turned out to be the kick I needed to get back on my feet.

I got my push bike out and started to go walking, using the bike as a crutch. I walked miles, forcing myself to go further and further each day, slowly building up my strength and my self-belief. And sure enough, two weeks later, I managed to get back to work.

However, it was never going to be as simple as that. I still could not walk without crutches, and I couldn't hold my spanners. I could no longer drive, so I had to take two trains and a bus just to get there each day, which with my health the way it was, exhausted me before the working day had even begun. Throughout this entire period, we were not offered any help or support at all. No medical assistance for my rehabilitation, no council or governmental allowances or benefits to ease the financial pressure. We were completely alone, with two young children and no money. It was costing nearly all my earnings just getting to and from work, and what was left over did not stretch very far. We struggled on like this for four months, by which time the children were going to school with holes in their shoes as we just couldn't afford new ones.

One day, as I was making the arduous journey to work, I slipped on the stairs at Harrow Station and fell. I missed my train and was late for work – and I was fired. This was the final straw for me, and I sank into a deep depression.

Twice during that time, I tried to take my own life. Twice, I had my stomach pumped to get rid of the overdose of pills I had swallowed. I just couldn't find a way of believing that life was worth carrying on with, and I felt I was a burden to my family; that they would be better off without me.

Despite my depression, I had at least one victory: I had learned how to control my right leg again and make it do what I wanted. I could now walk without help for the first time since the coma, and I went for long walks every day, unable to cope with being stuck inside the house all day. My walks became longer and longer, until one day I walked so far, I no longer knew where I was. I had been walking for several hours and had completely lost track of time and had no idea how to get home. I was exhausted from walking so far and needed to rest, so I sat down on a grass verge and fell asleep. I fell asleep regularly back then, and I have no idea how long I was out for.

I was woken by a lady asking if I was OK. I reassured her that I was fine, which I'm not sure she believed, and she offered me a lift home. Of course, I had no idea where I was, but I didn't want her to know that, and I knew I couldn't give directions to get back so I thanked her and walked away.

To this day I have no idea how I got home, but somehow, I did. Outside my house there was a police car – Jan had called them because I'd been gone more than eight hours and she was dreadfully worried. Of course, I hated all the attention and I found it very hard to accept her concern. We began to argue, and the arguments became more frequent and more intense. Every little thing triggered more arguments and we were both miserable. We still had no help – the GP gave no suggestions about how to get any support and even told me to pull myself together. It was a brutal part of our lives – one I cannot look back on with much pleasure.

The only positive at this time was the time I was still spending with my children. We sat for hours on the lounge floor with a deck of reading cards, putting them into sentences and practising our writing. They had no idea how much they were helping me, but without their knowledge, they taught me to read and write. I came on such a long way that I felt inspired to take an English course to get some qualifications, and I took my GCSE in English – and I passed.

I was so proud to have finally got this qualification, but it proved to be little help at that stage. I still couldn't get a job and was told when being interviewed for one that I was 'next to useless' because I couldn't stand well or hold a proper conversation.

My GCSE Certificate in English.

But something had changed in me. I no longer felt defeated by life– in fact, my resolve stiffened and I was determined to prove I was worth something. I had to stop trying to change and start dealing with life as I now was. I had to do something to help other people; show that I was capable of really achieving things. My local hospital, Mount Vernon, I discovered, was trying to raise funding for a new scanner, and this seemed to be the perfect reason. I knew I had to do something extraordinary to raise enough money, and it had to be something memorable. I wanted to show the world that my disabilities would not stop me, and so I came up with the perfect challenge to prove to everyone that I could overcome anything.

I would walk from Land's End to John O'Groats over 14 days.

Chapter Ten
Taking on the
Ultimate Challenge

People react to bad news in different ways. For some, being told they would never walk again would be the end. They might accept their fate and adjust to a new normal. I've never been one to take things lying down though; somewhat ironically.

Once I'd regained consciousness after the haemorrhage, I was in a pretty low place. I'd forgotten so many basics on top of the physical disabilities: reading, writing, fundamental fine motor skills had all gone. I worked with various physiotherapists to try to regain full use of my body while I was at Maida Vale hospital but I was never sure any of them really believed I'd ever do it. In fact, I think the only person who really did believe it was me, and even I had my moments of doubt. The physio then stopped when I got home until they saw that I had a different idea about my future. I was later told that the paperwork had been lost in transferring my care. This seemed to be the way with all the support we were supposed to have got, but I feel it was this that made me turn it all around.

I met some great people in those few weeks that I was in the hospital. Some of the memories are hazy now, but some are crystal clear. The guy in the bed opposite me who needed several enemas, poor chap; a young guy called Steve, who had a lump in his leg. It was cancer, and they amputated, but he died when he was 21. I sometimes wonder whether if he had his chance again today, he'd get to live longer, with all the advances in medicine since that time. But I suppose we'll never know. There was another young lad, Ricky, who was waiting for an operation. He was convinced he was dying (it wasn't hard to believe, he had blood coming out of his eyes!) and was desperate for a 'last meal' before his operation the next day. So, the first time I was allowed off the ward, he and I nipped up the road for a curry. Delicious it was too. For this 'outing' there had been some conditions set down by the ward Matron; a porter had to push the chair I was in and a nurse had to come along to look out for Ricky and yes, before you ask, he survived the operation – no idea what happened to him after that, but I'll always be glad we got to share that curry.

The children played a great part in the early days of my recovery. I'd watch the way they moved around, Emma toddling about with her nappy on, bumping down and clambering back up again in all sorts of ways. I started to copy her, using my stomach and hip muscles instead of my legs, because I couldn't feel them at all. My legs were like lead weights, I had to think a lot more about how I moved. For a while, I used a bright orange space hopper, rolling across it until I was able to stand up or crawling, crab-style, across the floor and walking my hands up the wall or the furniture to stand. I hated it, but it was working, and gradually I was getting my movement back, as well as my speech. Before long

I could move around almost normally by binding my knee to help me lock it – at least that's how it appeared to other people. Nothing felt normal to me, and sometimes I wonder if it ever has.

Many memories were gone, and some have never returned. There are some things I knew I'd done before the haemorrhage, like knocking down a shed in our garden and demolishing a load of concrete; I'd also rebuilt the bathroom and toilet and installed a new suite, built a dividing wall to make two smaller bedrooms out of one larger one, and decorated both. I could see that I'd done those things but had no memories of doing them whatsoever. It's a pretty disconcerting feeling. With work too, there were things I'd forgotten, basic skills I'd always had but which had now just disappeared, like changing a cam belt, or remembering which screws to undo when changing a carburettor.

The worst thing though was losing the memory of Emma's birth and all the appointments leading up to it throughout Jan's pregnancy. Russell's birth I still had – but Emma's seems to be one of the prices I paid. I do remember a few details – she was exceptionally hairy, a memory I'm sure she'd be happy for me to have let go of! But so many of those precious days have gone. At least I have been alive to watch her grow up though and for that, I will always be grateful, however tough some of those years have been. Sometimes I wonder whether we became closer because of it, as I spent so much time with her, relearning those basic skills, and making new memories that I was determined I'd never lose again. By Christmas 1983, I was walking but still needed a stabiliser to keep me steady. I used a pushbike because I refused to use a cane all the time. One night, a group of us went out for a few drinks, and we were talking about taking on challenges and raising money. One of them mentioned that a hospital near us, Mount Vernon, was trying to raise money for a new scanner. I realised that if I'd been sent to that hospital, without a scanner, I would have died. Immediately I knew I'd found the cause I'd been looking for. There was talk of organising a charity walk, from John O'Groats to Land's End to raise the funds needed, and I was convinced I could do it.

Of course, everyone laughed at the idea at first. I could barely walk to the end of the street – how on earth could I even contemplate walking over 600 miles? But my mind was set, and soon after that, I began to train.

I walked everywhere, and increased my distances at the weekends, way beyond what I knew I could do. I had to build up stamina, and my friends began to believe that maybe this would be possible after all. I kept at it and grew stronger week by week. We had spoken to the hospital, who were delighted with the support. Maida Vale hospital, where I'd been diagnosed, was less impressed and washed their hands of me altogether. The doctors advised me not to do it, but I stubbornly ignored them and carried on. The children loved the training, coming with me on lots of walks. It didn't occur to me until much later how much I was neglecting Jan at this point – every free moment was taken up with either training or planning, and I didn't make any time for her. She was desperately worried about my health, as I was going against all the doctors' advice, but I ploughed on anyway. Maybe I should have listened, but I didn't, and here we are today.

Support for the cause and my walk was growing in the community, and we were now getting a fair bit of attention and some generous sponsorships. That community support was what kept me going and fuelled my determination to succeed. A local sponsor had given me a tracksuit with my name on the back and I'd wear it on my training walks; people started to recognise me and cheer me on even at that stage. I would suffer dreadfully with cramps in my legs and on one of the training walks I stopped at Mount Vernon Hospital to get my legs looked at. It amused me that no one had a clue who I was, or what I was doing for them, until Dr White came down and got me sorted out. I had physiotherapy to help my cramp and build up my strength.

Not everyone was as supportive as I recall; one particular morning, I was walking towards work on Edgware Road and was stopped by the police. I had a CB radio with me, so I could keep in touch with my family and let them know where I was, and a few sets of keys, for home, for work and so on. This must all have looked highly suspicious to the arresting officer, who was convinced I was out to commit some kind of multiple robbery crime sprees. Why he thought I'd choose to do that with my name emblazoned across my back is anyone's guess – perhaps he wasn't used to a particularly high calibre of criminal! I was arrested; my boss had to confirm the keys really were meant to be in my possession, and my father-in-law had to come and bail me out – he was thrilled, as you can imagine. My boss at the time wasn't too please either – he wouldn't allow me more than my two weeks of annual leave to complete the walk, which put a lot more pressure on the timescale than I'd anticipated. But with the threat of losing my job, I had to keep to it. On the whole, though, the support I got was amazing. My friends had volunteered to be alternating pacemakers for me, and we'd arranged a caravan to live in on the road. But with just a couple of months to go before the walk was due to start, we came to a sudden realisation: we didn't have a car suitable to pull it! Through work, I had a contact at Daihatsu, who was one of our suppliers, and I told them about my challenge.

Unbelievably, they provided a red four-track vehicle to pull the caravan.

Admiring the view from the caravan at Lands' End on the night before the walk. This was to be our accommodation for the duration.

I'm grateful to them to this day. Nike donated six pairs of trainers, and a local sports shop donated socks, vests and shorts, all in red to match the Daihatsu.

The week before the walk started, Watford Football club allowed me to walk around the pitch before the match with a collection pot. Radio 2 had started recording for a half-hour program that was planned to be aired after the walk. There were ads in the local newspaper from businesses showing their support. The paper then donated all the money from the adverts to the cause, and other people started raising money off the back of it too, local pubs and so on. Before we even started the walk we'd raised a whopping £70,000 towards the £124,000 that was needed – it was incredible really.

Marathon man's lap of honour

ANDY Kent, the stroke victim who intends walking from Lands End to John O'Groats next month for the Mount Vernon body scanner appeal, received a warm round of applause and encouragement from Watford's football fans on Saturday.

Andy, from Rickmansworth, did a "lap of honour" in front of the 13,000 strong crowd before Watford took on Wolves in their First Division match.

He had been given a track suit, shorts, vest, socks and jogging shoes for his effort by the 'Not Quite So Perfect Charity Trust Gold Society'.

Andy is trying to raise as much as possible for the appeal only a year after he suffered a brain haemorrhage—and was saved from permanent brain damage by a scanner which pin-pointed his problem and allowed the right drugs to be administered.

At the moment he has promises of £4,000 but would like to have £10,000 pledged before he sets off on June 16. He can be contacted on Rickmansworth

Watford Football Club was a great help. They allowed me to publicise the walk on the pitch before a home game.

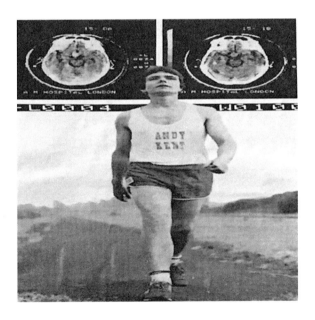

News cutting with brain scans.

So, the stage was set, the training was done, and the challenge lay ahead. 741 miles in 16 days – I must have been crazy. The target was 64 miles a day, walking for about 16 hours. I was determined, I was ready: I had no idea what lay ahead. The impossible was about to start or so some were saying. I had aimed to come across the country from Lands' End to Mount Vernon hospital and then travel up the country. Yes, this was the long route but I felt it was what was needed to make the statement.

On the 16th June 1984, we began walking. It started pretty well; all things considered. In many of the places we passed through, I got such a great welcome, it really spurred me on. But with the good experiences came the bad, some lorry drivers would flick their cigarette butts at us, some police constabularies did not want us to walk through their county. The cause we were raising funds for spurred me on. The cause was so close to my heart that it really kept me going, as did all the faith our local community had put in me. I didn't want to let anyone down – I wanted to be just Andy, not the hero, to forget that schoolboy and all the crap I'd been through.

Taking the first steps as we left Lands' End.

We had walked through the heat of the day getting sunburn and with all the training we did, we did not expect to get the blisters on our feet. The first leg up to home went reasonably well, we had managed to stay close to the target – within 12 hours of our target times. I had been relying on the other lads that were on the trip with me, John our driver and cook, and the two pacemakers that would walk with me to keep the pace that we had set out, to get to the setpoints each day.

Day one and we were already
getting sunburn.

It was great to see my children the day I got home but I made one big mistake. We had planned to go home via The Cross pub, a bit more publicity for the walk. The publican had arranged for some of the press to meet us there. All I could think of was my family when I got to Maple Cross, so I took the shortest route to them, missing out on the pub until later.

*My high protein diet, quick and easy and then just a few hours'
sleep.*

Because of the hours I was walking, I was by now
depriving my body of a lot of necessary vitamins and proteins
so, on our way through, we detoured to Mount Vernon
hospital for some advice and support with our diet and for
them to look at my left leg and back as they were taking a lot
of punishment. By this time, I was now getting blisters on my
left hand because I was having to use my crutches more and
more. But I was sure I was not going to quit.

Mid-way, at Mount Vernon Hospital.

But as the walk went on, it took its toll on me. By the end, I was down to 20 miles a day and behind target; I'd torn the ligaments from the left side of my knee and had to use crutches all the time. We crossed the Forth Bridge and I had to stop at a hospital in Kirkcaldy for treatment. The treatment I was given was second to none and once they had heard what I was doing, they gave me a set of old wooden crutches that they had all signed wishing me luck, for us to sell to help with the cause. However, they told me I had to stop, or it would be a very long road to recovery, but I ignored them even with my leg in a Robert Jones bandage (those of you that know what this is will understand the restriction of having it). I ignored them but within a day they were proved right and I had to quit. Day 14. I'd already rung my boss to tell him I was behind schedule; it was galling to have to call it a day. Ironically, had I not made my route longer in order to incorporate a visit to Mount Vernon Hospital in the early days, I could have made it.

As you can see I'm back on crutches. My left knee being the reason we did not quite get there.

We were so close; the fact remains though that we raised a lot of money towards the cause. £124,000 at the final count. The hospital not only got its scanner, but it also got an entire new purpose-built wing for it to go in. And that's what I have to focus on. The whole community treated me like I had done it and reached John O'Groats because the money was still raised, the awareness was there, and the scanner was bought. I had almost done it, and with my limited mobility, it really was an achievement to be proud of.

My fantastic helpers along the walk.

Yes! The cheque.

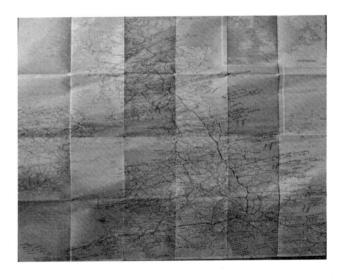

The route with some heart felt notes written along the way.

Chapter Eleven
The End of a Very Long Road
(and the Start of a New One)

Despite not finishing the last section of the walk, we had garnered a lot of media attention. We were fortunate to have some great support from BBC Radio 2, for which I'll be forever grateful. One reporter used to bring his Jag into the garage where I worked. Always one to chance my arm, I took the plunge and asked whether there was any chance he would help us move things forward and give it some coverage. He said he thought it would make a great story and things moved on fast from there. I got to know him pretty well, even visiting his house in Thetford a few times, along with Jan – we went for Bastille Day once! Then Gary Davies took the story on, over on Radio 1, and the coverage took off even more. I was on the radio, and there were lots of meet and greet events, including the one with Gary Davies to hand over the cheque to Mount Vernon hospital, which was quite a day. I was invited to Ruislip Fair, an event hosted by the mayor, and I was stunned when he presented me with the key to the town – one day perhaps I'll borrow some sheep to take to the market square to assert my right!

The day Gary Davies came to Maple Cross.

It was a lovely gesture, and I'd had no idea it was coming – what a great surprise that was. Another time, I was invited to a charitable dinner which Jan came along to as well. Dr Strickland attended too, the consultant from Mount Vernon Hospital, and Prince Michael of Kent. There was also an event where I was privileged to meet Princess Diana, a highlight I shall always cherish – she truly was a lovely girl. Despite all the excitement though, the main feeling after the walk finished was just tiredness. I was absolutely knackered!

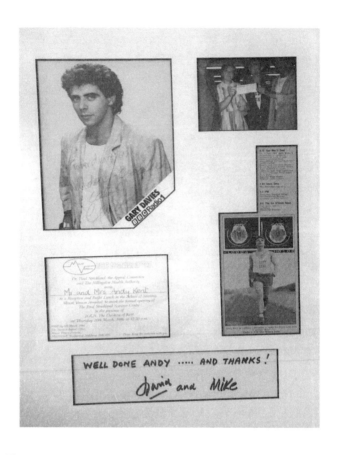

This memento was presented to me and proudly adorns my office
wall.

The initial jubilation at raising the money and attending
all the events where I was being congratulated and praised
soon gave way to other less positive feelings. Anti-climax.
Disappointment. Futility. Frustration. I had nothing to look
forward to now, nothing going on. I was struggling to come to
terms with the difficulties I had doing everyday things, like
holding a cup or writing things down. I relied on others to do

the work when I was at the garage, so all I could do was instruct. After the challenges and achievements of the preceding months, it was pretty hard to take.

I questioned everything. Why had I been allowed to live? What was the point? So many other people had died around me, including six others in our region alone from cerebral haemorrhages. (Seven people within a week all with the same issue, and I was the only survivor. There was blasting going on behind Maple Cross at that time for the M25 – I have my suspicions that the blasts may have been responsible, but no one can prove anything now. These days, this would have made headline news and been properly investigated). I couldn't really see the point in any of it or anything.

Trying to make the most of my time with Russell.

Russell in his little AA car

Spending time with my family was the only thing that helped, though there were strains there too – with Jan, and I didn't see how deeply my depression was setting in. I began to drink more and stopped taking the pills I was supposed to take, a combination of painkillers, blood pressure tablets, anti-epileptic pills and antidepressants. The spiral continued, the blackness got blacker, the future grew dimmer, and I didn't want to keep going.

One particular day, I started drinking a bottle of vodka early in the day. I kept going, and my resentment and frustration spilt out of control. I remembered my pills and began to take them until they were all gone, and then took every other tablet I could find in the house. Things got very hazy after that, and I don't remember much as I became delirious. But at some point, before losing consciousness, I told Jan what I had done. She called an ambulance, and they saved my life. It's not an experience I'd recommend, just for the record – being pumped full of charcoal to make me sick, and not just once, oh no. Several times, over and over, to make sure it was all gone. That was a bad day.

In my rational moments, I knew suicide was not the way to go. But I couldn't see any other way out of the situation I was in. The doctors kept telling me how fragile I was, how the slightest bump to the head could kill me. I couldn't swim alone, couldn't do anything on my own. Everyone was watching me like hawks and it was unbearable.

I started going out for walks again since that was the only way, I could get people to leave me alone. I loved that time to myself, to the point where I would just keep going for hours and hours. Obviously, this was before mobile phones or even pagers, so no one knew where I was. Jan would worry and call the police, or I'd sit down to rest on a verge and nod off and be woken up by some irritable policeman summoned by a concerned passer-by. It was a pretty dark time, no mistake about it, and I had no idea what would come next. I just walked and was returned home, a wannabe runaway with nowhere else to go.

I quit my job. I was working at Mann Egerton, a big dealership in Rickmansworth, which was fast paced and busy, but it was close to home so involved less travel. I was coping, just about, but I didn't feel like it, and my manager hadn't been at all supportive or understanding. Enough was enough. I left after just six months and got a job at Barlow Handling, a forklift company. I loved that job. I was my own boss more or less, free to go out on my own with no one checking up on me all the time. I could even take Russell out on jobs with me, and I became well known to the customers. I enjoyed the office life too and it was pretty close to home, in St Albans. I even had a van which meant I could carry my tools around with me wherever I went. I enjoyed being at work more than being at home at that point, and I spent more and more time away, loving my work. Sometimes I had to force myself to go home. Little did I know, the damage my absence was causing.

It started with rumours, people telling me they'd seen Jan with a friend of mine, that they'd looked 'friendly'. At first, I didn't think too much of it. Jan was faithful to me – sure, ours wasn't a perfect marriage, but we had the children, and each other, and we pulled through.

Until that is, Jan took the children and completely disappeared.

Chapter Twelve
Going It Alone

I'd lost my sense of future, lost my goals. I didn't realise I'd also lost my wife. At first, I ignored the rumours, laughed off the idea that she might have met someone else, that she would have an affair. I'm not sure if she'd have left if things had stayed the same. But they didn't. She got pregnant, and there was no hiding it anymore. Though at the time she left, I had no idea. I didn't work it out for quite some time, as it turned out.

On Friday 16th June 1986, I came home to an empty house. There was no note and all I could find missing were the children's toothbrushes and their coats – nothing else, other than a Morris 1100 I had just bought for Jan as a run-around. It was also an investment as it was an old one with low mileage.

If she had told me she was going away for a weekend, with the children, to see friends – just a weekend, I would have said "No big deal." Except, she hadn't mentioned it and there was no note. Friday 16th June 1986. I remember that day as if it were yesterday. I called her parents first, not overly worried, just a bit concerned; they said they had no idea where she was. I tried everyone I knew who might have a clue, but no one did. That's when I called the police, but it hadn't been long enough, so they weren't in a rush to act. I was frantic.

About a week after she left, with still no word, I remembered that she'd arranged, sometime previously, to collect her aunty Margaret from a convalescent home in Portsmouth. It's not like people had mobiles back then, and with her parents still saying they'd heard nothing, I decided I would go and collect her myself. I duly packed up the car, stopping en-route at my brother's to check he hadn't heard anything. Still nothing; he wound me up a bit though, as he'd heard the rumours about Jan having an affair and implied that she'd left me for someone else. Yet again I refuted it. "If she's gone off with some fella, I'll blow his bloody kneecaps off," I said as I left.

God, it was a long way to Portsmouth. I'd hardly slept in a week, and my eyelids were heavy on the motorway. As it was getting late, I stopped at a service station for coffee. I knew I must be tired since I couldn't even find the bloody exit – but after a couple of laps of the car park, I eventually figured it out (do they design them like that deliberately? Like it's a test of mental agility to leave them? The Bermuda bloody triangle of motorway traffic!) and was on my way again. But the coffee hadn't worked well enough and I knew I was in danger of falling asleep at the wheel. More worried about harming someone else than myself, I pulled into a layby not too far from Portsmouth and finally closed my eyes for a doze.

I was jerked awake by a loud rapping on the window.

"Get out of the vehicle, sir," said a surly policeman, pointing a pistol at me. That was a pretty unusual sight in 1986 – police didn't often carry guns, so it was even more alarming. I wound the window down but was again instructed to leave the car, which I did, though they made me put my hands on the car roof, making the whole thing extremely awkward.

"Remove your jacket," I was told. As it happened, it was the same jacket I'd worn on my walk, so they had my name already since it was emblazoned on the back. He was pointing the gun right at my chest and I just saw red – I grabbed the gun in his hands. "If you're going to shoot me, just bloody well shoot me," I shouted. "But at least tell me what it is I'm supposed to have done!"

The officer called one of his colleagues over to restrain me and told me again to remove my jacket. So, I did. They wanted the jacket off, they'd damn well have the jacket off – and the top, and the trousers to boot! So, there I was, standing in a layby in the early hours of the morning, stripped down to my underpants with a policeman pointing a gun at me, and still no idea why it was all happening. They clearly had no idea what to do with me but it must have been obvious I wasn't an immediate threat, so they told me to get dressed and arrested me. Only then did they ask what I'd done with the 12-bore shotgun.

"What shotgun?" I made it extremely clear that I'd never in my life owned a shotgun and certainly didn't have one in my possession at that time. They searched the car, which was (obviously) empty, and then took me to the nearest police station, from which I was transferred the next morning to Weymouth for questioning.

They put me in a cell with a guy I can only assume was an undercover policeman, since he seemed remarkably well informed about my circumstances.

It was another 24 hours before they got around to actually questioning me, in a relentless three-hour session. So, it wasn't until then that they let me in on what was happening – they knew, they said, that I had a gun with me because I'd threatened to go and blow someone's kneecaps off. (Gee, thanks bro.) I explained that I'd only said that to my brother as an angry figure of speech, that I didn't even believe my wife was having an affair, let alone going off to confront whoever it might have been with. They'd searched the service station car park apparently, obviously assuming I'd disposed of the gun while circling the car park… who knew getting lost could be so badly misconstrued?

At long last they allowed me to get in touch with Jan's uncle, so he could make arrangements for Margaret. Without any evidence after another 24 hours, they had to finally let me go – to make my way back to my car, which had been towed to Portsmouth police station for a thorough search, which meant it had been stripped completely and put back together pretty half-heartedly. Thoroughly miserable, furious and alone, I went home to my empty house.

The days dragged on into weeks with no word, and my mood got worse and worse. Alcohol became my go-to comfort, and I began drinking more by the day. I couldn't stand the idea of never seeing Jan or the children again, and the more I obsessed over it, the more miserable I became, and the worse my drinking got. By my birthday, the 21st of July, after too many pills and a lot of vodkas, I'd had enough.

Somehow, I managed to cut and strip back the wires on Jan's hairdryer and wound the bare wires around the toes on each foot. I lay down on the bed, and saying my goodbyes in my head, I plugged it in, switched it on – the pain was immense. In fact, it took me a while to realise that if I was still experiencing pain, it meant I wasn't dead, and my suicide attempt had failed. I'd hoped this would be a quick and direct result – no room for error with pills. I just wanted it over. Yet here I was, somehow, wretchedly alive. It took a long time to be able to even switch it off again, and my feet were badly burned. I felt like such an idiot when I realised why it didn't work. Had I attached the wires to my hands, so much closer to my heart, it might have worked. But as it was, I just ended up in agony, the soles of my feet burnt and blistered. I couldn't move. For nearly two days I just lay there, wishing I was dead and feeling like an idiot. During that time not one person came looking for me. No one wondered where I was, no one knocked at my front door or called me on the phone. I was totally alone. When I finally went to the GP about my feet, they didn't believe how it had happened. I still have the scars on my feet to this day. Still no real support, I was trying to kill myself and yet the doctor would not listen to me.

Was I going crazy? My wife had run away with my children, I'd tried to commit suicide, no one was helping, or listening, or believing what I told them. How had I got here? I have never intentionally set out to hurt anyone other than myself.

Chapter Thirteen
A Glimmer of Hope

I can't recall exactly when the phone calls started. Around 2am, jerking me from sleep. "Are you Jan's husband?" I'd be asked. "Father of Russell and Emma?" But as soon as I asked who it was, the line went dead. It happened several times – what had started as hope quickly turned to frustration and annoyance as it got me no further. Someone, somewhere, clearly knew something, but I was none the wiser.

I wracked my brain for places she could have gone. And then I had a brainwave – Blackpool! It was where we'd been when we were first getting to know each other and she'd always enjoyed it there. Perhaps Blackpool was where I needed to look. I enlisted the help of my solicitor and he managed to track down the road she was living on, though not the specific house number. I had photos. Photos which showed as well something I'd always denied... that Jan had left me for someone else. For someone else who had been a good friend of mine. This was the friend I had confided in; this was the friend I had helped to get a job and helped to support him and his family (wife and two boys) while he was looking for work. Even lending him money to see them through to payday on several occasions. I had to confront them. I knew my car would never make it as far as Blackpool, so I had to make arrangements for a new one. I let Jan's parents know that I'd found her and told them I was planning to go up at the weekend to see her. I roped a friend in to come with me and off we set. It took a while to find the street but find it we did, and then we waited, watching for a sign of Jan and the children. It was only later that I found out that speaking to Jan's parents was the worst thing I could have done. As it transpired, they had been in touch with her and knew exactly where she was and had been lying to me to keep her away from me. They warned her that I was coming to see her and encouraged her to move on before I got there. After thinking I was so close to getting her back, I was back at square one, although at least now I knew she and the children were safe. I drove up there as often as I could, trying to find her but never managing to track her down. I was desperate.

In early September I had a bad fall at work and needed yet another operation on my knee. In plaster, I couldn't drive for the rest of the month so my trips to Blackpool had to stop, but I received another blow courtesy of Jan's parents – both children were enrolled to start school in Blackpool. This was the final straw, and as soon as I was able, I drove through the night back up north to make one last-ditch attempt to find her.

I'd underestimated my exhaustion though, and the after-effects of my operation. The stitches tore, and the plaster was soaked through. I stopped in the middle of nowhere, down a farm track I think it was, to rest overnight. I got my pills and a bottle of vodka, which I began to drink. I must have drunk most of the bottle before I became desperate for a pee – so off I went to the back of the car to relieve myself in the hedgerow. I have no idea what happened then, but I obviously passed out, trousers around my ankles. What a sight I must have made. I woke up in the hospital, where I'd been taken by a police officer who, having seen the pills and vodka, assumed I had tried to commit suicide. It took a while to convince them I wasn't suicidal, and eventually, they let me go – although it took an age to find the car again since I'd been so out of it by the time I'd stopped, I had no idea where I'd left it!

In October, I found them.

I was walking along the prom in Blackpool and there they were. Russell spotted me first and sprinted towards me, throwing himself into my arms. I can't tell you how much I'd missed him, both of them, the smell of them, and their little arms thrown around me. I was so relieved to see them again. And that's also when I discovered that Jan was pregnant.

I knew immediately it wasn't mine. It couldn't have been – I'd had a vasectomy after the cerebral haemorrhage. It made sense, Jan had told me the Christmas before that she had wanted more children, but because of my health, we had to stop at two. Maybe that was one of the reasons she left… I don't know. But it was impossible to ignore the fact that she was pregnant now. I can't remember what we said to each other that first day. The whole thing is a blur. But I had found them, and I was damned if I was going to lose them again.

She agreed I could come and visit again. On the next visit, I went to the B&B where she was staying, and this time it was Emma's turn to greet me. I'll never forget the sight of her, standing at the top of those stairs and shouting, "Daddy, Daddy!" and running to me.

I visited as often as I could after that and after a few weeks, to my amazement, she agreed to come home. I couldn't believe it, after all those months alone, wondering if I'd ever even see her again. I don't know why she agreed to come back – maybe for the children, maybe things with the other man hadn't worked out. I didn't question her too closely and she didn't offer me any details. I just accepted her word and that was that.

Two days after she came home, she said she had to go back to Blackpool to "finalise her affairs." She stayed for a week, and I thought she'd changed her mind. To this day I don't know what she did in that week, but she came back home at the end of it and I have never asked. She was home, and we were together for Christmas, with our amazing children, and her big baby bump, a constant reminder of what had happened. But I was still just glad to have her back.

The day my children came home and started back at the local school.

The baby was born in March – a girl, Lynsey. I offered to raise her as our own, but Jan said I'd never be able to accept her, that she would always be a reminder of that awful time. Even now, things still go back to that time, and arguments circle back to her infidelity. I'm not proud of it – but it happens. Perhaps, I blame her. Perhaps, I blame myself. I really don't know. But the baby was put up for adoption and we said goodbye to her. The more I think about this now, the more I recall the words that were said during the months leading up to Jan going off in the way she did. I hope that one day Jan is able to talk about it. About the pain of giving up a child, about why she'd left, and why she came back. Or was she always going to come back? Maybe she blocks it out; maybe she thinks about it all the time. She won't speak to me about it and we have built a new life together, wanting to think that we are putting the whole episode behind us, but sometimes it surfaces again, and I know that Lynsey is still in her thoughts, at least sometimes. One day, Jan. One day. Some years later, at the first opportunity we had, we moved to Chatteris. We wanted a clean slate, away from the prying eyes and wagging tongues of people who had known us and our situation. Without the judgements and the preconceptions, we felt we stood a better chance of making it work. And it has worked.

I found employment not far from home, so I got to spend far more time with Jan and the children, and over time, we grew closer. The years passed. We don't have a perfect marriage, and we never had, but we have a marriage, and it works for us. We are lucky in so many ways. Sometimes it's good to remind ourselves of that.

Our first Christmas in Chatteris, 1993.

Chapter Fourteen
The Seeds of Industry

In 1996, I began working at Bar Hill Motors, developing my mechanical and managerial skills once more. When I started there, the owners weren't sure what to do with the place. The manager wanted to retire and business was far from booming. But by the following year, it was showing promise, and within three years we'd paid off all the debts and the business was turning a decent profit. I became a director and things were looking good.

By May 2001, my health had become an issue again. I had to go into hospital to have my knee replaced and it took several weeks for me to be able to return to work in any meaningful capacity. So, it was around September before I could go back and by that time the business had deteriorated significantly. It was looking doubtful we would meet our targets, and there was talk of selling. I did what I could, and we limped along for a few more months, but I knew trouble was brewing and it wouldn't be long before it came to a head. The talk of selling became more frequent and I started to wonder whether I might be able to buy them out and take over.

I asked the other directors for the first refusal on the place, I said I'd try my best and put in a competitive offer. A higher offer was put on the table but they said if I could get to within

10% of that, the business was mine; but they wouldn't tell me what the offer was, so I was bidding blind. I talked to the bank, to my solicitor, anyone who could help me raise the money to buy the place. Against all the advice I was getting, I put in my very best offer and hoped against hope that they'd see fit to sell the business to me. Later, I discovered that the business bidding against me was owned by a friend of one of the directors. So, while at the time it was a surprise that they rejected my offer and went with the other company, it very soon made perfect sense. The new owners came in to meet us; I had a feeling things were not going to play out well, and I was already seething with resentment about being passed over after my years of loyalty and turning the business around. And I was right. I was, as they told me in no uncertain terms, surplus to requirements. Their managers were quite capable of running the place without me, thank you very much, so I would have to work in the workshop. With my health and physical ability issues this wasn't really a viable option; I suppose I played right into their hands. I gave up my directorship and focused on the holiday I had booked with the family.

But what they didn't know was that before I went, I had been scouting out another property. It was a nice little premise just around the corner, and the day I got back from our holiday I got confirmation that I would be able to get planning permission to do engineering works on site. That was all I'd been waiting for – I marched into work my first day back and handed in my notice. I offered to work my notice period but they paid me a severance fee instead and I left that day.

I worked my arse off that month, painting and decorating and using up savings to get all the equipment I'd need to set up the rival garage. My old employers tried every trick in the book to shut me down but we opened Andy's Kars on 2nd November 2002, and I can honestly say I have never looked back.

Chapter Fifteen
Andy's Kars

I won't pretend that running my own business has been a walk in the park. Far from it; the responsibility, relentless workload and incredibly long hours have been tough over the years. But the sense of achievement, of seeing something that I started growing and flourishing – well, that makes it all worthwhile.

With Richard, a friend at the time, the day we opened Andy's Kars, 2002.

The early days were stressful, of course. Just getting set up was hard enough, securing the premises and getting it all kitted out, especially after the somewhat acrimonious split with my former business partners. We had a few customers, people I'd known and worked with over the years, and word seemed to spread fast. I've always taken great pride in my work; whatever I would be paid for a job, it would always be done to the absolute best of my abilities, no matter how long that might take. But good workmanship and great service are sure-fire ways to win loyalty, and I found that people were coming back time after time. I have never stopped adding to my knowledge and skill; it's a continuous process for me, and that's something I've always insisted on for my staff and family as well.

I always liked the idea of Russell and Emma one day joining the business but I didn't want to just hand them a job on a plate either; for me, it's important that people work hard for what they want, that they get out in the world and get qualified, gain experience, and make their own way. There's a lot of life out there to understand and get to grips with. And not just for experience either – I wanted to know that working here was something they really wanted and hadn't just fallen back on as the easy option. Passion for your work is so important – if you don't love what you do, then you're probably not giving it your all or doing it justice. Working should be something that creates funds for you to have a reasonable life outside of it. To have the time to spend with your family and friends, to be able to take your family on at least one holiday a year and be able to live with something left over at the end of the month. I have always believed that to obtain this you should aim for the highest level you can achieve, without forgetting those around you, who love you.

When we started out, I suppose we were a pretty standard garage, but we quickly gained a reputation for doing things properly and giving great service, with a spin. From day one, I said that we would employ and train people that found it harder to get work than the mainstream applicants. We fast built a reputation for employing young people with challenges.

Even doing everything I could, I was always pushing the boundaries as to how long I could keep going.

We would get the occasional customer approach us, who had a disability of some description or other, and I always really relished those cases. We were starting to get a reputation for recognising difficulties and taking the time to find solutions for people with individual needs. It gave me the chance to really think, to use my mechanical skills and my understanding of physical capabilities to create customised solutions that helped people get their independence back. Nothing was more satisfying. It was a side-line at first, just something I dabbled in, but over the years it's grown from minor fixes to full vehicular adaptations. Word spread and more and more of those cases would come along, and the business has become more defined by our adaptations and accessibility than anything else. I find that side more rewarding than standard mechanics because it's all about the individual. To a completely able-bodied person, having a car is a bit of a given, just something you'd expect. To someone with a disability, however, it can be totally life-changing, opening up opportunities that may never have been possible or returning someone to independence whose health had previously taken it away.

Just after Russell joined the business, back in January 2005, we were contacted by Motability. They wanted us to do some fault-finding work on vehicles, which we duly did. They were pleased with the work and came back to us more often. Over a period of three or four years, we worked on extensive research and development to identify and rectify why certain faults were recurring. Based on those findings, they changed the entire code of practice on how to manufacture, install and adapt equipment, working to much higher standards and introducing better training for accredited mechanics.

Of course, as a result, we were getting less work from Motability – shooting ourselves in the proverbial foot! As there were fewer repairs, however, they suggested that we started installing the equipment in vehicles ourselves, so we became accredited, and have never looked back. The scale of the work we can now undertake has moved on dramatically, and a big part of that is thanks to evolving technology.

There are so many different medical conditions that can affect a person's physical and psychological abilities, that very few cases are ever the same. From stroke survivors to those with muscular restrictions, people with impaired vision, loss of limb or neurological conditions like epilepsy; few businesses take the time to consider the ramifications for those people when it comes to transportation. But thanks to technology, things that we could only imagine 20 years ago are now possible – and who's to say what might become feasible in the next 20 years, what with self-driving cars, voice activation and things that haven't even been invented yet.

The widespread use of electronics in cars these days has opened up a wide range of possibilities. Having mainframe computers that control so much of a car's functionality might seem a luxury to those able to perform basic tasks themselves, but for people with limited or inconsistent movement, it can be a real game-changer. Simple changes can make a big difference; lightened steering, for example, can make driving a pleasure again for people with muscular restrictions or frozen joints. But of course, "simple" changes for the end user are not simple for the mechanic, with knock-on effects with ABS systems, tractions control, etc. So, although electronics have made some things easier, it has made others far more complicated, so the need for constant learning and development is ever-present.

Andy wins award for success in the automotive business

A LOCAL charity's founder has led by example and gained an academic qualification at the same level as a Phd, despite having to overcome a disability.

Andy Kent, who founded local charity Andy's Ark, which aims to provide training, support and qualifications for disadvantaged and disabled people in the motor industry, has been presented with the Automotive Management Accreditation, level seven in senior management.

The accolade was granted to Mr Kent, who also owns Andy's Kars, Bar Hill, and is the first of its kind, designed to acknowledge the management training required to run an independent or franchised dealership garage.

Andy graduated from the scheme along with managers from national firms including Autoglass, Jaguar Land Rover and Scania.

He said: "I am thrilled to be given this award, it shows that you really can do anything given the opportunity.

"I left school at 14 with very limited reading and writing skills, to a level that meant that no one expected me to achieve more than a manual job that needed a high level of support.

"But I went into the motor trade as a workshop assistant and very quickly showed that there was more inside my head, and that given the opportunity I would be able to become a motor mechanic.

"Shortly after completing my apprenticeship I had a stroke, at the age 24, leaving me with physical and mental disadvantages, but I've tried to never let it get in my way. This is always something I try to teach our students. I always strive to act as a role model for them.

"If you have a dream hold on to it and work to make it come true. It's your dream and it is up to you to make it work for you. It does not matter how you get there, just do all you can, it takes some of us a long time, others make a lot quicker."

DREAM COME TRUE: Steve Nash, BMW director, left and Andy Kent

It was very nice to be recognised within my own trade.

We can now undertake almost any type of adaptation, but not with an 'off the shelf' solution. Every person we see, has unique circumstances and I make sure that what we offer them is right for them, suits their needs, their abilities and their lives. Whether that's accessibility, hand-controls, voice activation, in-car harnesses, adjusted steering or visibility aids, or any other modification, we always assess the individual's needs rather than simply fobbing them off with a ready-made answer. I sometimes think society sees the less able-bodied as a drain on resources; yet by helping people to regain their independence, I hope we are offering them a way back to a rewarding life. It's not just a car we are changing – it's a life.

Chapter Sixteen
Changing Lives

I made a conscious decision early on, largely based on my own experiences in life where I felt I'd been so held back and penalised for my education and health. I wanted to give people like me the opportunities that no one else would offer them. So, I made a point of hiring people with challenging backgrounds or circumstances, people who perhaps had found it difficult to gain employment elsewhere, or who had physical or mental challenges that made work more difficult for them to find. I started taking on apprentices and training them up, teaching them the mechanics, the service side, and the business skills to take forward.

It wasn't a formal arrangement at first but the more people I welcomed through these doors, the more people I saw change in front of me. As they grew in confidence and started to believe in themselves as I believed in them, the more I realised that this was where my life's work was leading me. This was where I could make a difference. On the one hand, giving customers their independence through mechanical and electronic modifications to give them their freedom; on the other, to give young people the opportunity to make something of themselves, to learn skills, gain qualifications and earn a living for themselves when they'd never thought they could. I've never forgotten the feeling of being told I would never amount to anything, of being that child in the corner with the dunce's cap on. If I've saved one person from feeling that way, it's all been worthwhile.

There's still a stigma associated with disabilities, as there is with mental health. I'm heartened, in many ways, to see the advance and awareness gathering pace, but even now there's a long way to go. Occasionally, we'll still get the odd customer who thinks we won't do a good job because of our circumstances. Our bodies may not always work the way we'd like them to, but our workmanship has always been second to none, and the vast majority of our customers know that. I remember one particular customer getting so irate because we'd had the audacity to let a woman work on his car! He threatened to take his car elsewhere as a result – and funnily enough, I agreed that, that was much the best idea. There are some people whose minds I'll never be able to change, but I will never stop working to challenge the stigma around disability and mental health. I know first-hand how many lives have been transformed simply by someone believing in them, by trusting them, by empowering them through knowledge, skill and opportunity. Sometimes it really is a case of that one chance that can change everything. If I can be that chance, no matter what, I'll take it.

It was because of this work that I decided to set up a charity to raise funding and awareness. Andy's Ark was established in March 2009 and became a registered charity in 2013 and is to this day, one of my proudest achievements. It's up there with my children and their children.

The aim of Andy's Ark was exactly what I'd already been working towards – to help local people with challenging circumstances get qualified and help equip them for independent, successful lives.

Challenging Attitudes - Changing Lives.

Charity aims to offer a helping hand

A CAMBRIDGE charity will run a course to help women cope with their troubled motors this winter.

Andy's Ark, a charity which helps disabled and disadvantaged people into employment, will run the course.

Charity founder Andy Kent said: "Many women don't know what they need to do to keep themselves safe in their cars over the winter months. This course, which is designed to be fun and informal, will show you

Charity founder Andy Kent is keen to help women motorists.

how to check oil levels, windscreen wiper fluid, tyre pressures, among other essential pieces of mechanical knowledge."

The course begins on October 9.

A local newspaper ran a story, 2010.

It wasn't easy, the road to getting it founded and recognised. It took a huge amount of work and commitment and support from other people to help raise funds. But we did it, and I will never regret it, not ever.

It breaks my heart that just five years later, I had to close the charity down. The reasons are complicated, essentially boiling down to petty, bureaucratic issues that shouldn't have such a bearing on such a worthwhile cause. Sadly, some of our trustees are no longer able to offer the support or vision that originally helped make the charity such a success, and with various other factors in my life, I just don't have the energy or the resources to keep it going. But I will never stop working to further the cause I believe so passionately in, and which I know has touched and enhanced so many lives.

We've met some amazing people over the years through Andy's Ark, and I'm so proud to see so many of my lads and lasses go on to find rewarding and successful careers elsewhere. We even had a young guy who went on to be a Paralympic gold-medallist – I'd like to think that some of that resilience and mental toughness was learned at a little garage just outside Cambridge. Some of the people who have been through our doors have been kind enough to write and share their experiences of their time with us, so I've included some of those at the back of this book. It means more to me than I can say to read those words and see how they have flourished thanks to simple self-belief.

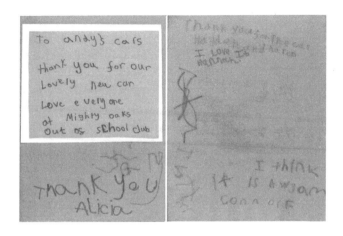

Some of our visitors were local school children. This is a card we received after one such visit.

Working in this line has given me some great experiences as well and I've been lucky enough to work with some wonderful people. Some of them have shared my vision and goals wholeheartedly, and I've often been deeply touched by their recognition. The work I've done has led to some awards and nominations of which I'm enormously proud and am always grateful to have a wider platform from which to spread the word of challenging stigma. I don't seek awards or recognition, but when these things happen, it's a wonderful chance to talk to more people about the importance of independence and freedom for all lives however challenged they may be.

The challenges, they come and go

I'd love to report that, since opening Andy's Kars and founding a charity I was so very passionate about, life calmed down and I could just enjoy myself. And to be fair, there have been so many happy times in recent years that it does make up for the challenges we've had to meet along the way. But sometimes, I wish that someone up there would just give us a break.

Not many years ago, we moved to a lovely new house. Because of my own physical issues, we had to spend a lot of money making the house fully accessible for me, and it took a long time to get everything just right – stressful enough in itself. But other issues were at play as well; we had run-ins with a neighbour who made life very uncomfortable for us and seemed to take issue with our – or more specifically – my very existence.

Again, this was a family that we had helped and offered support to during the early years. Giving the children a tent that our children had grown out of. Taking the guy to rugby matches because he did not seem to get out. I was also asked to witness their parents wills when they moved back to Spain. Paying for a digger so that we could do our front gardens over the same weekend because they could not afford it. For the first ten years, we seemed to be good friends. Then it all changed when we had to replace the fence between our two properties because their dog had run through it plus it was getting to that stage when a replacement was in order. Even after all the good times we had enjoyed, we could not agree on where it should be, so it was removed.

We could do nothing right; we parked in the wrong place, we made too much noise, we had too many workmen on site. We even had the police called on us, on more than one occasion – oh, did I mention that the adults were both police officers? Unfortunately, that all escalated into an extremely unpleasant and protracted two years of immense distress and upheaval. They were using their position in the force to threaten me. I was even arrested at one point, dragged to the police station in the middle of the night, sustaining injuries in the process – of course, all this was taken up with the police to no avail but, the upshot was, we were made to feel so unwelcome in our own home that we ended up throwing in the towel and moving again. At the time I was furious that we had to move. So much time, effort and money had gone into making that house just the way we wanted it and needed it to be and here we were, moving on again before it was really finished. But the house we're in now, we love, and so as with so many things in life, it has all worked out for the best, even if it didn't feel like it at the time. The drama of those two years took a heavy toll on my health though, both physical and mental, and it was an extremely difficult time for all of us.

However, something happened to turn all that around, and that something came in the form of yet another little miracle, our grandson Archie. I've mentioned before that my family has been plagued with ill health. Not just me; I've already said so much about that. Jan too has had more than her fair share of issues, and my poor, brave daughter Emma, who has battled through more operations than she should ever have had to bear, who has repeatedly defied doctors' belief, who has no stomach left and who should by all accounts not be able to have children – Emma, had a son. Archie was born on 18th July 2017.

The next generation. Like his mum, a miracle baby.

It seems somehow fateful that Emma had her miracle baby. After all, I was told I couldn't have children, yet had two, and now my daughter, who by rights shouldn't even exist, who was told that she too would not be able to conceive, defied the odds and brought Archie into the world safe, healthy and happy. He has brought so much joy into our lives, so much energy and innocence and hope. He's a living reminder every day that no matter what fate throws at you, however out of your control the events of your life may seem to be, you always, always have a choice. You can lie down, accept defeat and give up. Or you can stand up, put one foot in front of the other, and make the very best of whatever it is you have. The grass is never greener on the other side of the fence. It may look that way, but we all have to walk or crawl or wheel our own roads.

I've had so many worries over the years, worries that my children would inherit my health issues. I remember when Russell was about 12 and we had to rush him to the doctor's because he was in pain when he had to have a pee, and when he managed it, there was blood in it. "Here we go," we thought, and a nervous future of health issues and hospitals flashed before my eyes, making me feel guilty for ever having children. But fortunately, it turned out to be some kind of crystals forming in his bladder which were easily treated and he went on to be perfectly healthy. He gave us our first very special grandchild, Imogen, on 4th July 2011.

Like her father, she's a bit of a monkey, always swinging around on climbing frames and the like, and we could not be prouder of her, nor love her more.

So, my parting words to you, kind reader, who have taken the time to discover my life, my mishaps, my escapades and my struggles, are these: don't give up.

There is always a way, and life is always worth living – and living to the full.

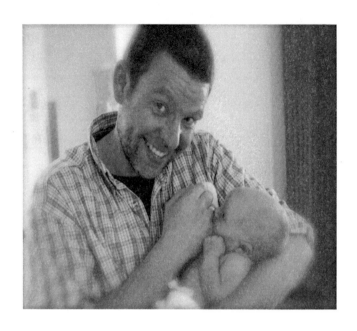

Our first miracle was Russell so, seeing him become a father, too, was overwhelming.

Be kind, be loving, be fair. And above all – be yourself. Because no one else can ever do that for you.

Chapter Seventeen
Contributions from
Other People

It's not what you know...

Whatever challenges I've faced in my life, it has always been the people around me who have made it worthwhile. I am honoured to have had the opportunity to work with some very special people. When I decided to write this book, I got in touch with a few of them and asked if they'd be willing to share any memories or thoughts about our time together. The next few pages are a collection of those shared memories, by people I feel very lucky to have crossed paths with.

Michelle Barrett

I've worked with Michelle at the IMI for many years now and was truly touched by her words. Thank you, Michelle, for taking the time to write this, and for all your hard work and support over the years.

From Michelle Barrett, Ba (Hons) Mimi
A lasting impression

I'll never forget meeting Andy for the first time. There I was, in the car park, just before an IGA meeting where I was representing the IMI, wrestling with armfuls of stuff, when he appeared, offering his help. I couldn't help but notice his difficulties in movement, yet he was only too happy to help me out. Inspired and humbled is how I remember feeling in that moment, and that impression has never left me in all the years I've known Andy.

I was a national manager at that time, supporting motor industry businesses. I was just blown away by Andy, both professionally and personally, and he continues to impress and inspire everyone he meets to this day.

In the beginning, I got to know Andy through the business, but the more we chatted, the more I started to find out about his background. I couldn't get over what he has managed to achieve in the face of unbelievable adversity; yet through his health challenges, personal struggles and hard work in business, he has remained so positive and so generous to others and so incredibly gracious. You can't help but be inspired when you speak to Andy. He's just that sort of a person.

The consummate professional

Andy is, and always has been, an absolute professional. He always gives 100% in his service and engenders that same respect for everyone who works with him so, the whole business reflects those same values. He's helped so many people, given so many opportunities to young people and made such a difference in other people's lives. Andy has always been dedicated to helping others throughout his whole life, and it's amazing to see the business he has built from the ground up so dedicated to improving challenging lives, giving people back their independence, and all through doing something he loves so passionately.

Given the difficulties Andy had at school – he was barely able to read and write by the time he left – it's incredible to look at what he's achieved. His technical knowledge and ability are outstanding. He absolutely flew through the Master Technician accreditation, which is the highest standard of technical competency in the industry. And as if that wasn't enough, he then went on to achieve the highest level of the Automotive Management Accreditation (now known as the IMI Accreditation of Management). It's a tough accreditation to get, and a lot of people don't make the cut. Andy was actually something of a guinea pig for that programme but again, that's typical of Andy – he's always, always ready to help out, and devote his time to causes he feels passionate about.

This was an award I had never expected I would get, to me it was about others.

He's always been a big supporter of the IMI. He's helped out in so many ways over the years, from drafting letters for us to the skills council and local government, advising on technical alterations and new developments. His industry and mechanical knowledge really is second to none and the expertise he brings to Motability adaptation is industry-leading. He's now a Fellow of the IMI, an accolade, usually only achieved at a postgraduate level of education; it's an astonishing achievement given the education he started with.

Well-deserved recognition

There's absolutely nothing mercenary about Andy; he's always got something to give and it's always driven by kindness and wanting to help other people. But it's not often Andy gets given anything in life, so I'm always pleased when I look back at some of the awards and recognition he's earned over the years. I've been lucky enough to attend a few of the awards ceremonies where Andy has won and have nominated him for some awards over the years too. I remember the Barclay's Trading Places Awards in London, which was such an inspiring evening it brought more than a few tears to the eye. To this day, I can't remember what I said but I know he deserved every second of appreciation. In 2015, he won the inaugural IMI Award for Outstanding Individual Achievement and again it was an incredibly proud moment as I watched him accept his award. Sometimes it seems so unfair, the challenges he has had to face, and yet he's always smiling, always helpful, and always, unendingly kind.

Over the years of knowing Andy, I've also got to know his family, especially Jan and Emma. It's been such a rewarding experience to know Andy, and I'll always be grateful to him for coming to my aid that day in the car park. He's an amazing person, so kind, and so inspirational. He's made so much difference to so many lives – both personally and professionally, he's definitely one of the best.

Nathan Missen

Nathan was a very special lad who I remember very fondly. I had the pleasure of working with him some years ago and watching his transformation is still something that makes me tremendously proud of him. After his tragic death, I kept in touch with his father, Dave. When I told him about the book, Dave was kind enough to write to me about Nathan, and I wanted to share his words with you here and thank David Missen, Nathans father for his support of the Andy's Kar, Charity.

Dave Missen's Contribution

I first met Andy when my son Nathan started going to Andy's Kars on a day release programme from Cottenham Village College. Nathan suffered from dyspraxia, so had difficulty with a lot of physical movements. He struggled with school and lacked confidence and belief in himself.

The gift of a bright future

Nathan started going to Andy's Kars one day a week. It was meant to be for about three months but ended up being far longer; Andy had arranged the scheme with the school to help youngsters. It was such a great idea; giving kids practical skills and experience they could use. I used to pick him up from Andy's occasionally, so I got to meet him then.

My impression of Andy was that he was someone who knows what he wants, and who wanted to help others. He certainly helped Nathan, giving him as much technical know-how as possible and helping him to gain masses more confidence in the motor trade. Nathan loved it there – he even went during the holidays sometimes, which he got into trouble for, but he got so much out of it.

Andy and his team gave Nathan the chance to believe that he could do it, and really helped him when they saw he had a genuine interest in the work. He was young, so there was a limit to what he was allowed to do, but Andy helped him as much as possible and taught him a lot. Andy helped a lot of kids like that – kids that the school system wasn't helping. We definitely noticed a real difference in Nathan after he started going to Andy's – it was a great thing to see.

Thanks to what he learned with Andy, Nathan was able to go on to become a trainee fitter with Kwik Fit and was looking forward to a great career in the motor trade. Sadly, that future never happened.

Nathan was tragically killed in a car crash on 19th August 2010. He'd been off visiting his girlfriend, who he was really excited about, when it happened. It was an awful time for the family.

Inspired to make a difference

I felt I had to do something to help Andy after Nathan's death – he'd done so much for Nathan and I wanted to help him in his quest to make a lasting difference in other people's lives. I signed up to run the London Marathon, in 2012, for Andy's Ark and was amazed to raise over £6,000. I did some other charity events with Andy after that too and as a team, we raised enough money to help make Andy's dream come true – Andy's Ark was given charitable status. I couldn't believe we'd done it – it was an amazing day.

Nathan at work.

I'm so grateful for the way Andy helped Nathan and am really pleased with the work we did to get Andy's Ark the charitable recognition it deserved. I just wish Nathan had been around to see it.

Andrew Youle

Another bright spark I've had the honour of getting to know over the years is Andrew Youle. What a difference to the young lad I first met all those years ago; Andrew's achievements make me enormously proud, and his determination and perseverance are an example to us all. As I knew I wouldn't get a word out of Andrew himself, I cheated and asked his mum Karen to tell his story. And here it is.

Karen Cook On Andrew

Andrew was first introduced to Andy through the Cambridge Regional College, which secured him a placement as part of the course he was doing there. We were both nervous about how the placement would work out, and things hadn't always been easy for Andrew.

All his life, Andrew has found it difficult to talk to people and interact with them. He finds people really hard to read, so is never sure how he's supposed to respond. Unfortunately, his dad found this very hard to deal with and didn't really support him in his early years; we're no longer together, but I remember it being a difficult relationship for Andrew. Andrew has had a tricky journey through life, being in special schools and having such difficulty communicating and dealing with people. As a result of all this, he had extremely low self-esteem and some complex emotional needs. As is often the case with a "hidden" illness, he looks completely normal on the outside so people find him harder to understand, as they don't realise how difficult he finds things, and that he doesn't always know how to react in the "right" way.

On Andrew's first day at Andy's Kars, I can remember both of us being very nervous. This was Andrew's first contact with the real world of work and I didn't know what to expect. I remember telephoning Andy because I was deeply worried, but Andy was so reassuring and told me he knew how to work with Andrew, and that it would be fine.

Since then, we have travelled a long road together, through good and bad times. For example, thanks to Andy knowing a driving instructor who would be exactly right to teach Andrew, he was able to pass his driving test on the second attempt. He's also been able to develop his skills as a mechanic and is now a fully qualified MOT inspector. I'm so proud of what he's achieved, and how far he's come, and I'm so grateful to Andy for the time he has put in helping Andrew to really find himself.

The changes in Andrew aren't just at work. At home, he feels more valued and contributes more. He still struggles now and then, but because someone like Andy believed in him, and gave him the time to complete tasks at his own pace, his confidence has grown and he has become so much more independent. He now feels able to talk to my husband if he has a problem, which is a big thing for Andrew, and he's much happier in himself, much less frustrated and fed up with himself.

Without Andy's intervention, I don't believe Andrew would be where he is today. Andy is a very modest man; whenever I've tried to thank him for what he has done for Andrew, he just tells me it was all Andrew, not him. But it was Andy who gave him the help and guidance he needed and believed in him and made him believe in himself too, showing him that the sky's the limit. He helped me too, to let go a bit, and give Andrew the space and independence to make his own mistakes and deal with the consequences himself. I never expected Andrew to be able to achieve so much after the difficulties he had at school in his early life, and a lot of that is down to Andy's care and understanding. So, thank you,

Andy – you're a star, and you've changed my son's life beyond belief.

Nathan Carter

Nathan's story has a double bonus in it for me; not only was I fortunate enough to be able to help Nathan himself, but his mum Nikki has been a long-term acquaintance too and is now a highly valued employee here at Andy's Kars. Both Nathan and Nikki were happy to share their memories for the purpose of this book, and it means the world to me to see their stories here.

Nikki's Contribution On Nathan

I was given Andy's number by a lady who was making my son's 16th birthday cake. We'd been chatting, and I mentioned that I was trying to find a work experience placement for him in a garage. My son had severe dyslexia, dyspraxia and auditory memory loss so, it wasn't easy to find somewhere that would be suitable – and she told me about Andy, and Andy's Ark.

From the first time I spoke with Andy on the phone, and he told me about his own challenges and what he'd gone through, and continued to live through every day, I knew there was some hope of a brighter future for my son, thanks to the work Andy was doing with the children at Andy's Ark.

That summer that Nathan started working with Andy, I saw an immediate change in him, all for the good.

Unfortunately, my own health had started to deteriorate, and the company I was working for at the time and had worked with for 26 years, was becoming very difficult. I called on Andy's amazing knowledge of working and employment laws for the disabled, as I desperately needed advice.

I had a meeting with Andy and he told me how it was in plain and simple terms. He even offered to come to the meeting with me! I was so grateful to have someone who I knew was on my side and wasn't going to let anyone pull the wool over my eyes. Just him being there provided immense support and some hope for my future. Later, I needed his help again, this time with the adaptation of a vehicle, as by this time I needed to use an electric wheelchair more and more. Andy showed me all the adaptions that could be fitted to cars to help me stay independent and mobile. Yet again, Andy showed me that there is always a life out there no matter what your circumstances, even for the less mobile. Andy also recommended cars that were more suitable for hoists. Sadly, my sporty car days would have to end, but at least my driving days could continue for many more years.

Around two years later, I received a phone call. It was Emma, Andy's lovely daughter, asking if I might be looking for a new job – I think perhaps she'd been chatting with Nathan who had told her how unhappy I was in my current position. She had certainly caught me on the right day! I went in for an interview with Andy the very next day and a month later I started working with the team at Andy's Kars, and I can honestly say I've never looked back. Having a boss who understands your challenges and will make allowances for them, is extremely helpful. Andy is always very caring and made sure that everything I would be using was right for the particular challenges I had, and that they were comfortable and safe. He understands that people have off days – that some days are harder than others when a particular challenge flare-up. I love working with Andy, and the whole team. Seeing him working with customers with challenges and seeing their faces when he tells them there is a way for them to drive again is the best thing ever – and you can see how happy it makes Andy as well. Andy gave my son a brighter future when no other options seem available, and he gave me the chance for a new working future where I could be happy, mobile and independent, just when I was beginning to think there was no way forward. I'm so grateful to Andy for everything he has done – I wasn't ready to give up work, and now I know I don't have to. Thank you, Andy!

What Nathan Has To Say

I never really enjoyed school. I found it difficult as I have severe dyslexia, dyspraxia and auditory memory loss; even with the help of a teaching assistant, it was always really hard.

My one great love in life was cars, and I so wanted to get a job working with them somehow. I had tried to get work at many places but just kept meeting a closed door. Then, on my 16th birthday, I got home to a double surprise – a fantastic birthday cake, and the news that there might be a chance of some work experience at a garage!

That's how I met Andy. I spoke to him on the phone, something I would normally have found very difficult, but Andy really put me at ease. He invited me over for an interview, and I actually started to get excited about a possible future.

I went over to see Andy and he explained to me about the work he had done with other children like me through his charity, Andy's Ark. He offered me work experience to go alongside the college course I was going to be doing, and I was delighted to accept.

So, in August 2013, I started work experience at Andy's Kars. I would cycle from my home in Cambridge to Bar Hill, no matter what the weather. The guys in the workshop all took me under their wings and started to show me how they were fixing the vehicles. Andy would show me things too and explain things in a way that I could understand. He would also give me a list of spellings of garage items, terms or words that I would need for filling in job cards, and Emma helped me learn them, and would test me on them to make sure I remembered.

I continued working at Andy's Kars for the first year of my college course. With the help and support I got from Andy during that year, I passed my first year – and then Andy offered me an apprenticeship! I was absolutely over the moon.

Over the next few months, Andy showed me lots of different ways of fixing vehicles, while I continued with the second year of my college courses. I was finding college hard, as the TA I was supposed to have, was never there, and I was beginning to struggle with the coursework. I didn't want to admit I was struggling though, so I just kept quiet – but then came the exams. I hated exams. So, I did the stupid thing of just burying my head in the sand. I started to get moody and withdrawn. The final straw was being wrongfully accused of speeding on college grounds – that was it. I'd had enough. I was ready to throw it all away, but Andy wasn't ready to give up on me yet.

He spoke to me, and showed me how far I had come, reminded me what I had already achieved and how skilled I was becoming. And then he decided to teach me himself, showing me the adaption side of the work he did, which I took too quickly and seemed to have a real flair for. I really enjoyed learning about electrics, welding, fabricating and modifying vehicles.

Andy never gave up on me. A few years later, in December 2017, I had an urge to try a new job in car recovery work. Although Andy said he didn't want me to go, he said that if it was what I wanted, then he would wish me all the best. Within four days in my new job, I realised that the grass was definitely not greener on the other side of the fence. I was doing 24-hour breakdown callouts, working six days a week – and I absolutely hated it. I had made an enormous mistake; I missed my "family" at the garage and even the work itself.

I rang Andy and admitted I'd made a huge mistake and asked if there was any chance I could come back. He asked me to come in for a chat. He'd already replaced me in the garage – but he still took me back. I had never been so happy or relieved in my life and had learned a serious life lesson.

From that day, I felt like I'd really grown up, become an adult, and taken control of my life. Without Andy and his family's help, I would never have managed to do what I have achieved; no one else was willing to give me a chance, and I have an awful lot to thank Andy for. I'll always be grateful to him for the start he gave me in the working world and is still giving me now.

Thank you, Andy – and remember, the grass is not always greener on the other side!

Emma – Andy's Daughter, June 2018

My dad: a hero to many, but who will always be my daddy. As a child, you never really know what is going on;

you just bumble along in your bubble, not really seeing or knowing what is truly going on around you or seeing the big picture. This was me. As a child, I didn't really understand why Dad did things differently or what was going on. As I've grown up and experienced things first-hand, I've understood things better. I've come to realise how amazing my parents are and appreciate them and what they have done for me – especially now, with me having my own family and health issues.

I love you both and appreciate you more than you realise, or I tell you.

Anyway, I'm meant to be talking about my dad. Daddy: the man that has gone through so much but still has warmth in his heart. Yes, we have had our bad times, but thanks to our stubbornness – (mine grown from him, Ha! Ha! Mum will love me blaming you, Dad) – we've worked through them and come out stronger for it.

The memories of my childhood that stick in my mind of Dad... where to start. The earliest is of sitting on his lap and snuggling in for a cuddle and getting confused as to why he didn't hug me back. Russell later explained that Daddy did love us, he just couldn't cuddle us very well at the moment, but we could still cuddle him. Dad was/is always warm, so even if his arms aren't working, his warmth made it OK.

Next was being in Blackpool. I have two distinct memories of this time. One was seeing Daddy's car parked up and Russell stopping me from running across the busy road and nearly getting knocked over. The next is being stood at the top of the stairs and Daddy being at the bottom with open arms.

I have random memories of Dad going off from our family holiday for an interview. When we could, Dad would take Russell and me to work with him. I remember getting his sales team from one job in trouble with him because they were playing office chair races down the corridor with us, not answering the telephones!

We did a lot as a family, which has set the stage for how I am with my family now. As I got older, my dyslexia started becoming more obvious, and the college wanted to test me. I was mortified. I thought I was a failure and an idiot. I did the test, and it was confirmed, but they said there was nothing they could do to offer assistance as I had coped and 'hidden' it so well. I already was using the coping strategies they suggest. I hadn't realised I did things differently. I went home, completely unsure how my parents would react, but to my delight, Dad told me he was too, and they both said they were so proud of me and impressed that I had found ways around it. Even they hadn't realised. It turned out Russell was as well; whether seeing Dad and Russell struggle had spurred me on to find a way around things... I don't know. I was now given extra help and managed to pass my theory test. It was another proud moment for me, as we couldn't work out why at home practising, I could pass every question but in the test room, I failed. It was because, at home, Russell read the question and tested me; in the room, I had to read it myself.

As I hit my late teens, my health started to be an issue. No one really believed me until I had to stay in the hospital and then ended up having major surgery to remove my large bowel. My stubbornness again; I want to prove that I could go on regardless, a tendency which comes from Dad, I'm sure, after all, that I've seen him do and go through.

Growing up, there was a house rule: if you were unwell, you didn't go out with your friend and play, but if you were well enough to do that, then you could go to school. I carried this on, and if I wanted to go out with friends, then I damn well went to work to get the funds to do it no matter what. Hence, when it came to it, no one realised how bad things were. One regret I have in having this mindset is that it caused me to miss a very important moment in my dad's life. I missed the opening of Andy's Kars. I was, and am still, gutted I wasn't there. I had begged and pleaded with the Doctors to let me home or even just go on day release, but I had complications that at the time were confusing them so, they wouldn't let me go. Ha! Ha! Oh, how I'm like my dad! This was a big blow to me. I wanted to be there for Dad to support him and show how proud I was and still am to this day. I'd been trying to prove my fitness, to be let out, but I was harbouring a two-litre pus-filled abscess within my abdominal/pelvic area due to an issue that happened during surgery. It was finally found and drained over the course of weeks. Due to not making it, while I was off ward at another scan, Dad and Mum had snuck in and put the balloons from the day all over my bed. It was such a surprise – but not as much as on another occasion, I came back to my bed to find a massive Piglet sat there waiting for me! Mum later told me that Dad had seen Piglet and said he had to get him to cheer me up. This was my first proper stay in the hospital. I spoke to Dad most days sobbing, but he encouraged and supported me. I never gave up or in.

I finally joined Andy's Kars in January 2005, where more operations and bad health followed me. With each deterioration, the doctors would be in disbelief that I was still working. My response would be, 'Have you met my dad? Giving up isn't an option.'

Thanks to Andy's Kars, I met the man of my dreams. And true to the saying, he is like my dad in some ways. (They will both hate me for saying that!) We've had our rough patches but having seen what Mum and Dad have gone through and how they've stayed strong, we've not given up on working at it. Our little family was completed with the birth of our boy; again, like Dad, it wasn't meant to be possible, but thanks to the determination of our son, I enjoyed pregnancy and ten months of remission from my challenges.

Sometimes the lessons of a dad to his daughter are hard and painful, but he has always been there, encouraging and supporting me. I'm so proud of him and his achievements. I get cross and worry about him when he overdoes it, but like Mum always says, 'You'll never change him – and would we want to?'

Dad, you're a stubborn old git, but we love you and look forward to making lots of memories with you and your grandchildren. Dad, thank you for being you and making me who I am.

Emma with the little miracle boy, Archie at 15 months.

Jan Kent – June 2018

Well, Andy, you were right. Andy's words to me in those early days were that, as time went on, "You'll grow to love me." And I do, so very much.

It's such a big, big shame l didn't realise that when I left. I just wish I could turn back the clock, for those months I wasn't around, and I wish so hard that I could just wipe them from the universe and make it, so it had never happened. Now, and for always, I will hate myself for it, for making such a big mistake in our lives and almost throwing so much away. But I can't change the past; it's happened – what's done is done. But if I could take that time out of our lives, I would. The life we have now – together – of course, we have our ups and downs; who doesn't? But I still wouldn't change you, and I'm so sorry I took away your trust in me.

Jan's words written in the sand, 1992.

In the beginning, for the first years of our relationship and our marriage, I always thought two years was all I'd have with Andy. That was back in 1975 – and we're still going today, in 2018, married for 43 years.

We have two great children, now grown-up – Russell and Emma. We have two grandchildren, Imogen and Archie. We run our own business, still with the family; we have a great home out in the countryside, and I wouldn't change a single thing. We're so very happy now; it's heavenly.

As a family, we have always had health problems on and off, but it is just what we have been dealt with in life. We have lots of challenges and hurdles to get over, and every single one we overcome, we get through, and we move forward. Andy has always given his all, in many different ways, to love and care for his family and colleagues.

So, in this final note, to end this record of life so lovingly lived, I want to say this: NEVER change who you are, who we all are. The grass is NEVER greener on the other side. And as Andy would always say: I can, and I will.

JAN

Chapter Eighteen
My Family

As I hope has become obvious in the pages of this book, no one in the world is more important to me than my family. They are my life, my reasons for living. Reading their words here gave me quite a lump in my throat, I can tell you. Thank you, thank you, thank you, my wonderful family. You are my world.

Andy's letter to his family, August 2018.

It has been my close family that has been my backbone over the years, with their close and ongoing encouragement and support for me to strive towards my goals in life. This, therefore, is a huge thank you to them for being there for me.

Just before my last bleed and I was still able to take risks. Jan and I on a Submarine, Summer 2006.

JAN. My wife. You have tried my patience and my beliefs over the years but have also shown your love for me as it has grown. You were only expecting to have to put up with me for two years, and it's been over forty so far, and who knows how many more. Yes, we had six months apart during our seventh year as a result of that first bleed. Why? I'm not sure I really know, even to this day. It really tested our belief in each other, but I truly believe it has only made us stronger in the way we think about and respond to each other. I believe I would not be alive today if it were not for you. Over the years, for want of better words, you became my right hand and my rock. The early days were when you had the biggest influence over my health, as this was when I really started to believe in my can-

159

do attitude – and it was all because you told me to give it a go and had nothing to lose. Thank you from the bottom of my heart.

Our 38th wedding anniversary, November 2013.

Russell, my son. I may never have told you this, but I'm sure you know how very proud of your achievements I am. While your early days at school were very trying for you academically, you always enjoyed football and made it onto your junior school Saturday team. Your academic side only really came together when we moved up to Chatteris for the last two years of school – and then on you went to university, and got a degree in Electrical Mechanical Engineering, which coincided with you getting an apprenticeship with the Environment Agency. You had some small health worries in your younger days, but you soon showed us how you bounced back. You have given us two amazing granddaughters – Faith, in Ireland and Imogen, who we love regularly seeing at weekends with you. Your work and input since you joined us at Andy's Kars have been invaluable. As with all fathers and sons, we have had our moments to laugh, our moments to shout, and of course, our moments to cry. Thank you – just for being my son.

EMMA, my daughter. Again, I may have taken it for granted that you know how proud I am of you and your achievements. Daddy's little girl, for whom the school was never easy; the reading and writing was there, but you never enjoyed it, and it was years before we found out why: dyslexia, just like your father's. That said, your maths skills were always second to none, as long as there was no reading involved! You went on to get a degree in accounting and got a job in quantity surveying. Like with your brother, we have had highs and lows as you found your own way through life, but you're still Daddy's little girl. Your health issues, which I wish I could take away from you, only really started at about eight when we noticed that you couldn't really chew your food properly. Your mouth was too small for your teeth, and something had to be done. You were so brave, having to stay in the hospital to have your four back teeth removed under general anaesthesia. But with all the other health issues you've experienced, you have always had the ability to bounce back, to fight, to the point where you've been here to support the family and the business, and against all the odds, give us a wonderful grandson, Archie.

Thank you, Emma, for being my daughter.

What is love? It's something that, when you have it; you know you have it. It's unmistakable. I hope all three of you know how much I love you and my grandchildren.

Along the way, there have been a lot of people that have helped me to keep going to get back to work each time things went pear-shaped, from the hospital staff at the many, many hospitals I have attended over the years to my friends and family. This book has been collated as a thank you to all of you. Most of you will know who I'm talking about, but for those who are unsure, please read the book again, and it will probably jog your memories, as writing this book has jogged mine. I must apologise – the part of my brain that remembers names is somewhat fried, and on top of that, I'd need a toilet roll's length of paper to mention all of you individually. But hopefully, you know the roles you played in this story that still goes on, and so to all of you who have played a part and crossed my path, I'd like to say thanks. It's been one hell of a ride.

High days and holidays

Barbequing in the garden for the family, a family camping holiday.

Admiring the steam engines with teenage Russell.

I have been fortunate to meet several 'famous faces' at award ceremonies and dinners. Here are a few of them…

Jan and I get up close and personal with the FA Cup at the Barclays.

I met Nick Hamilton in 2018 at the Commercial Truck Show at the NEC.